... mouth

... faith you

you and

... in your eyes

such a blessed

the Tears shall

... ...

... –

... ton

... think

... I adore

Ton Albert
qui t'adore

Violet Oakley
1928

Ton Albert qui t'adore

the courtship letters
of Albert Spalding
to Mary V. Pyle

Edited by
Suzanne Spalding Winston

Phoenix Publishing
Canaan, New Hampshire

Spalding, Albert, 1888-1953.
"Ton Albert qui t'adore: courtship letters of Albert Spalding to Mary V. Pyle" / compiled and edited by Suzanne Spalding Winston.
p. cm.
ISBN 0-914659-36-7: $22.50
1. Spalding, Albert, 1888-1953 – Correspondence. 2. Spalding, Mary V. Pyle, d. 1970 – Correspondence. 3. Violinists – United States – Correspondence. I. Spalding, Mary V. Pyle, d. 1970. II. Winston, Suzanne Spalding, 1913- . III. Title.
ML418.S7A4 1988
787.1'092'4 – dc19
[B] 88-19527
CIP
MN

Printed in the United States of America

Contents

Foreword

In the fall of 1970, I found the Vuitton steamer trunk in a third-floor storeroom at Aston Magna, exactly where I had seen it last. It had crossed the Atlantic with my uncle, Albert Spalding, on his concert tours more than one hundred times in three decades. Now it and several others of various sizes and shapes were serving as safe storage and sturdy reminders of the days of constant but leisurely travel, at home and abroad.

Mary Spalding lived on at Aston Magna for nearly twenty years after her husband's death. On my frequent visits during those years, she often reminisced about their courtship and their eventful life together, talked of their many shared interests, and showed me stored mementos and treasures. I remember vividly the day she opened the Vuitton steamer. We were in the storeroom, going over linens and Paris gowns. Throwing back the lid of the capacious old trunk, she revealed the stacks of neatly bundled and labeled letters she and Albert had written to each other almost daily whenever they were apart. The letters went back to the romantic days of summer visits between Monmouth Beach and Bernardsville, early in the century.

"What should I do with these?" Mary asked me plaintively. "Should I destroy them? Who would be interested? What do you think?" I remember wanting to comfort her, but all I said was that they were very precious to her. Only she could decide.

My unspoken thought was how valuable those letters would be to a biographer. Albert's own autobiographical memoir, *Rise to Follow*, on which I had worked with him, ends in the late twenties. Here was a priceless record of at least twenty-five more years of his concert tours, his war experiences, his observations on events, places, and people. More than once I had asked him if he wanted to bring his memoirs up to date. His answer was always, emphatically, "No!" World War II had changed his life and altered the world so radically that he felt he could not look back to the thirties and forties in the same way he had looked back on earlier decades. Besides, he was immersed in research on the life of Guiseppe Tartini. His novel based on Tartini's life, *A Fiddle, a Sword, and a Lady,* was published shortly before his death in the spring of 1953.

Aston Magna was dismantled after Mary Spalding's death in 1970. Some of its contents, most notably their collection of Oriental objets d'art, went to the Berkshire Museum in Pittsfield. Personal and professional memorabilia of Albert Spalding's career as a concert artist were given to the Mugar Library at Boston University for their Special Collections. They form the core of a major exhibition from September 1988 to April 1989, commemorating the centennial of Albert Spalding's birth.

The letters in that trunk numbered more than two thousand. Mary had already begun to destroy her own letters: today only those of the 1930s remain. Albert's letters were first transcribed by me in order to comprehend their scope and interest. I hoped, together with a musicologist, to compile and publish a record of America's first violin virtuoso of international renown – a man of unique qualities of heart and mind and spirit. Time did not permit the completion of such an extensive work by his centennial year. Instead, this little volume of the last six months of his letters to his betrothed following the 1918 Armistice, on the threshold of their life together and the unprecedented heights his career would attain, is dedicated to their memory with my love.

My heartfelt thanks go to Dr. Howard Gotlieb, the director of Special Collections at the Mugar Library, Boston University, whose friendship and encouragement over the fifteen years we have worked together on the Spalding archives have been invaluable. To Anne D. Lunt I owe special thanks for her expertise and inspirational help in editing these letters as well as many others on which we have worked together. May our collaboration and friendship long continue. My husband, Oliver

Winston, has given his quiet and strong support at all times, for which I am most grateful. My thanks also to the several friends who have read early drafts and strengthened my resolve to have Albert Spalding rediscovered. An important ongoing legacy is the Albert Spalding Violin Fellowship at Boston University's School of Music.

The proceeds from the sale of this book, after costs, will go toward the funding of that fellowship, established in 1953 and still growing. It is awarded every other year, for a period of two years, to a promising American violinist. The fellowship makes available a program of intensive study in preparation for a major performance career.

Suzanne Spalding Winston

Lyme, New Hampshire
March 15, 1988

Ton Albert
qui t'adore

Prelude

"Albert Spalding—America's first great instrumentalist." Walter Damrosch, conductor of the New York Symphony

"Mary Pyle . . . has beauty, sense, dignity and great savoir faire." Countess de St. Maurice, in Paris

THESE ARE THE LETTERS of Albert Spalding to his betrothed, Mary Vanderhoef Pyle, written during the final six months of a prolonged courtship. A warm friendship, based on many shared interests, had blossomed seven years earlier. Love was declared and marriage intended. Both families intervened with strong objections. The pursuit of his concert career must take precedence. His early and brilliant successes did not assure security or stability for marriage.

When America entered the war in 1917, Spalding enlisted in the Air Service of the Signal Corps and served as executive officer to Captain Fiorello LaGuardia in the Italian campaign, and from Foggia they undertook a crucial secret mission into Spain. Before he sailed, he had a reunion with Mary. All family restraints were overcome. They assumed the war would soon be over and they could then be married. Unfortunately, Mary's wartime letters have not survived, but Albert's reveal what difficulties lay ahead.

Both families were tenth-generation Americans with multinational roots, recognized members of the cosmopolitan set that divided its interests and activities between Europe and America. The Spalding name was synonymous with American sports. In 1876, Albert Goodwill Spalding, a former pitcher for Boston and Chicago, with his brother, James Walter Spalding, and his brother-in-law, William Thayer Brown, cofounded the firm of A. G. Spalding & Bros., to manufacture and

Casa Spalding, Lungarno Vespucci, Florence.

sell sports equipment world wide – the very first company to do so.

In the 1890s Marie and Walter Spalding established a winter home in Florence. They purchased the Palazzo Tallyrand on the Lungarno Vespucci and renamed it Casa Spalding. Their two young sons, Boardman and Albert, firmly guided by their pianist mother, began serious music lessons. Adolfo Castagnoli was Boardman's cello instructor; Ulpiano Chiti, a good-omen hunchback, was Albert's violin master. The two musicians were considered the finest teachers in Florence. Albert's talent for the violin was immediately recognized. Boardman diligently progressed with his cello in order to complete the family trio. With their mother at the piano, there were daily chamber music sessions. The boys attended the Franco-Italian day school on the Piazza Ottaviani, near Santa Maria Novella – the only American students among boys of various nationalities.

At Florenzia, their summer home in Monmouth Beach, New Jersey, the music studies continued with Juan Buitrago, a gentle South American who had been a protégé of Edward MacDowell. When MacDowell died, Buitrago came to live permanently with the Spaldings, sailing back and forth with them to Italy each season.

Albert's early choice of a concert violinist's career was a shock to everyone except his teacher – and his mother. Chiti confidently guided him to his examinations at the Bologna Conservatory, where at the age of fourteen, with a near-perfect score, he received a "professor of music" degree. Only once before had the conservatory awarded its diploma to one so young: to Wolfgang Amadeus Mozart, 133 years earlier.

His mother, Marie Boardman Spalding – an accomplished pianist, harpist, and singer who before her marriage had performed with the Chicago Symphony – had believed in him from the start. To others, however, for a young American boy from a well-to-do family to pursue music professionally seemed totally unsuitable.

America had hardly begun to be aware of the arts. Some homes were adorned with European paintings and engravings, and a few wealthy collectors were buying under the guidance of Bernard Berenson and other self-styled experts. Music, opera in particular, was chiefly a social event. Musicians, imported from abroad, were "entertainers"; often expected to use the servants' entrance. A few notable soloists were booked into American halls in major cities only after much acclaim abroad and avid promotion by some New York entrepreneur. All were

Marie Boardman Spalding, accomplished musician, and mother of Boardman and Albert Spalding.

foreign born and foreign trained. How could a young American violinist possibly succeed?

In his 1943 memoir, *Rise to Follow*, Albert says:

I have often wondered about my father's rather difficult role through the years of my musical development. It must have been at first trying, and finally alarming, this headlong pursuit of a profession so alien to his own business career, and then regarded as of doubtful masculinity. I cannot recall that he ever, by word or action, opposed it and it is with a certain wonder that I pay tribute to a great and broadminded pliability toward something that he must have sensed was inevitable. He it was who insisted that, until I should become self-supporting in my chosen calling, there would be a general tendency to regard me as a dilettante. With this in mind there was little to be gained by giving so many concerts in large cities at a loss, when you can be heard elsewhere and be paid for your work—even if only a pittance.

In the summers, on the Jersey shore, the Spaldings were curiosities to their neighbors. The sporting-goods aura was understood and the largesse of "A. G." and "J. W." toward the local boys' ball teams up and down the coast was accepted enthusiastically. But the Spalding "summer cottage," with its Italianate decor, liveried servants, foreign cars, tennis court with trellised arbor, acres of vegetable and cutting gardens, and formal Italian courtyards contrasted sharply with the casual life-style of the neighbors. The rigid daily routine of elaborate luncheons, afternoon teas, formal dinners, and evening musicales, attended mostly by out-of-town guests, musicians, and friends from Europe, was not understood at all.

Florenzia was nearly always full of guests. The Pyles, from Oakdene in Bernardsville, New Jersey, were among the frequent visitors.

The Pyle name, too, was well known. The public identified it with the diaphanous nymph on the packages of Pyle's Pearline, America's first nationally distributed and advertised soap powder. The company, founded in 1851, began its advertising when Horace Greeley's enthusiasm for the product and his friendship with James Pyle, Sr., led him to offer a year's free advertising in the *New York Tribune* to prove what advertising could do. After the founder's death, his two sons,

Albert's study in Casa Spalding.

James and William, carried on the thriving business. William, who was Mary and Scott's father, died in 1906, at only forty. His astute and beautiful widow, Minnie Vanderhoef Pyle, took charge and managed the family accounts so well that she was able to provide every advantage for her son and daughter. Scott was encouraged to pursue his art studies with the best masters in America and Europe. Mary studied at The Brearley School in New York. The family made "grand tours" to Europe, Egypt, and England. Prolonged stays in France and in Germany helped Mary to fluency in both languages.

Scott Pyle was a close friend of Albert Spalding. The two youths and Mary frequently exchanged visits between Florenzia and Oakdene and had a circle of gifted friends, including Tom Achelis, an aspiring actor; Luba d'Alexandrowska, an accomplished pianist; and several young painters. The young people followed up their visits with regular and voluminous correspondence. Mary and Albert soon discovered a mutual delight in books and art and spent happy hours reading aloud, discussing their favorite authors, comparing tastes in art and drama, and exchanging small gifts of books, art, and music. The first evidence of romantic overtones in the friendship is a note from Mary to Albert in July 1907:

Albert dear—I feel so wonderfully, vitally alive today I must let off a little pencilled enthusiasm. I might almost be a Nietzsche woman if that estimable seer ever thought of the ladies in his role! Tom [Achelis] *left me your volume of the Wagner controversy. What amusing and clever "harangues" they are from this old Titan of power and hate, and how ridiculously true many of his statements are altho' I have nearly caught him in a few inconsistences. What do you think of his estimate of your beloved Brahms? Are you not conscious continually of the insanity of the man, perhaps that is too strong, rather the warning, the approach of an unbalanced state. . . . Why do you not write me what you are doing, thinking, planning? You do send me occasional thoughts, don't you, my dear? Yesterday, I positively longed to hear you play, I am thirsting for some of your music. . . . If, by any chance you love me a little you might tell me so. I should love to be loved like a gust of wind today!*

The next letter found is from Albert, dated September 17, 1908, more than a year later, written aboard the *Kaiser Wilhelm II*. The

Minnie Vanderhoef Pyle, Mary's mother.

Scott Pyle, Mary's brother.

reference to "chère Cléopâtre" refers to a photograph he had sent her of herself costumed for one of the dramatic soirées at Oakdene.

There is quite a dull grey atmosphere outside and the ocean wears a cold, cynical appearance, but thanks to you, chère Cléopâtre, I can escape to my room where all is clothed in sympathy and warmth, what with the beauty of a stately Egyptian princess looking forth at me, with the charm of Mary Pyle's personality, and the interest I can now have in perusing Arthur Symons' books. I should have written you from Sandy Hook but . . . for the desire to see the last of great New York—so lovely seen from the harbor with its Whistlerian touch of haze and mystery. . . . When I at last descended to my cabin and found your packages, the mail bag had already gone ashore.

Many, many thanks for the charming books and still more charming photograph. I shall search far and long in Paris for a suitable frame. I have read little of Symons' books . . . . I quickly turned the leaves to his essay on Walter Pater, for I am at the present moment fairly "bristling" with Paterism, and was glad in reading it to find Mr. Symons also an ardent admirer of our dear writer . . . . I am still under the influence of that delightful afternoon's reading just one week [ago]—*when we*

Mary Pyle, "Chère Cléopâtre," costumed for an Oakdene fete.

were all together enjoying the scenes and the quiet landscape — "the ship appearing in full sail around the cluster of trees or over the garden wall where least [we] *might expect it." Could we not read it all together some time again? The beauty of it can never appear less beautiful for there is that simplicity of style, even when his writing is most obscure, of which one can never tire . . . . I shall go religiously to the Fall Salon and try and instruct myself to appreciate this wonderful man Cézanne with his new style, but when I want some true enjoyment I shall take my* Imaginary Portraits *and go to a quiet corner in the Louvre and look at Watteaus. And shall send you a picture postal of one of his dancing, fairy-like figures. That is, if you are fond of Watteaus? And how am I to know if you like Watteau unless you send me two words at the Athenée Hotel to acquaint me with your likes and dislikes in painters?*

True to his word, on October 16 he posted an envelope from the Carlton Hotel in London with seven Watteau postcards from the Musée du Louvre, with a brief message on each.

The New York music season of 1908-1909 opened for Albert Spalding with his debut with the New York Symphony under Walter Damrosch, who had heard about him directly from Camille Saint-Saens. As he had at his Paris debut four years previously, he played the Saint-Saens B-minor Concerto, followed two days later by the Tchaikowsky. That season also marked Toscanini's first appearance at the Metropolitan Opera, with the great singers Destinn, Sembrich, Eames, Farrar, Caruso, Scotti, Amato, Didur, and Witherspoon. Gustav Mahler was chief conductor of German operas. Arthur Rubinstein had had his first American tour in 1906. Mischa Elman had made a spectacular debut earlier in 1908, but Fritz Kreisler was the reigning prince of the violin.

Immediately after Albert's orchestral debut, he launched his first concert tour in America, with more than sixty appearances. In January 1909 he gave his first solo recital at Carnegie Hall. At this time, too, he signed a contract with Edison, which remained in effect for twenty years and numbered more than one hundred recordings. Later, he recorded briefly for Brunswick, then for Victor RCA, Remington, and Discopedia.

From 1908 to 1913 Albert and Mary exchanged letters regularly, expressing their growing affection and many shared interests. He freely accounts the particulars of his concert tours in Europe, Scandinavia, and Russia. When she traveled with her mother and brother in England and on the Continent they sometimes planned to meet en route, or arranged visits with his family in Florence, or extended their stay in Paris, if that was his headquarters.

In the spring of 1909, Spalding plays his last concert of an extended American tour and reaches New York just before Mary and her mother and brother depart for Europe. He writes that he can only be consoled by the hope of her coming to Florence in the winter. "I want to look at Botticellis with you and Scott. And have some long motor rides around olive-crowned hills." Later that summer, when she is in France, he writes:

We speak of you all often, and think even oftener (if I may judge from myself); to have you away is to have some essential and lovely instruments drop from our symphony of friendship! . . . When are you returning home? This last is a most interested question for I am not sailing as soon as I thought, I shall have concerts to keep me busy until far into November. Shall you be home, do you think, before then? . . .

Have you motored at all? Will you go into Touraine, or into Normandy? I think possibly one turns to [Normandy] *more in the summer than even that dear old Loire region. What a country of pastels France is! . . . Have you ever read "Les Lettres de mon Moulin" by Daudet? If you have not, hie you sur-le-champs to the nearest booksellers . . . . I know of no one who would appreciate and enjoy this little gem more.*

There were no meetings or visits in the summer of 1909 while the Pyles were in Europe, and no letters are extant except one in early fall, when he writes to Mary in England begging for the date of their return to the States. In early February of 1910 he writes her from the Grand Hôtel d'Europe in St. Petersburg, where he is on his first concert tour visit. His accompanist there was Raoul Pugno.

This wonderful Petersburg chains one's thoughts completely . . . . However the memory of some charming hours come hauntingly upon me — a cheery red drawing room, our brilliant hostess busy over a singing kettle and "over the teacups" shall I say? we discuss Pater, Symons, horrible man this last, he fascinates me and irritates me at the same time, the splendid performance of Tristan we so enjoyed together,

Isadora Duncan's dancing, Emmy Destinn's singing—tho' you never would admit to her lower notes being fine, you know *you wouldn't! Mary Garden's latest scandal. . . .*

Have you been to Russia, Mary? If so, you surely have never forgotten the Giorgione, the most splendid one for me, but then I must confess that it is some time since I have seen the one at Hampton Court. The picture here is of a full-length figure of Judith, and of such superhuman beauty that one almost—not quite but almost forgets one's ideal, the Mona Lisa. She stands bathed in a golden atmosphere, the serenity of nature and sky vying with that marvellous composure which is hers. The deed is done, but she feels no horror in the act, only a sense of supreme relief and freedom and her breath comes more easily. The entire composition sings the same note of (as the Germans would say) "morgenschön" and liberty, the only sober and tragic feature being a great dark tree which stands at the right—in respect to Death. What has Italy, or Italian art to do with this Russia, this Russia half barbaric, this country half hidden in night, and snow, and bowed down under a pessimism so strong that one cannot help feeling the influence. Indeed! I am sure that another six weeks of this life and I shall become the veriest pessimist and cynic that ever disgraced this beautiful world—what place has joyous Italy in this land of sadness? Raphael? Bosh! Giorgione? Pshaw! I must have bombs! I must have riots!—and the next moment I shall run to the other extreme and demand on the contrary "encore, encore!" of the wonderful fêtes, dinners, etc., the magnificence of which is really too overpowering. There is a rude and semi-barbaric grandeur in all they do—one must admire even if one does not approve.

The life is dreadfully taxing—the day commences never before eleven—I am considered early because I arise at this hour car vous comprenez j' ai mon travail, moi! *Then after two hours practise I take a sleigh and drive and drive on the Neva—sometimes on the ice of the river itself, and oh! the enjoyment of it, the flying snow, the horses half-maddened with excitement and biting cold, dashing at quite a wild pace, the brilliant colors of the liveries and uniforms standing out in such bold relief from the "gris-brun" atmosphere that is habitually on this city. Then to eat, and how I do relish the good caviar, the sterlets, etc.! Then a bit more music—then theatre, or opera, or perchance I'll plead guilty to a concert!*

Midnight soon tolls, and with every bell ringing, people seem to brighten and assume a mad gaiety none the less fascinating because

Florenzia, Monmouth Beach summer home of the James Walter Spaldings for four decades.

it is unnatural—perhaps a troika is ordered and a wonderful drive is taken to the Island, to Christovsky's to supper, it is really a thousand and one night's drama, and I shamefacedly admit that I love it, late hours and all! However, only a week more remains to me and then I must hurry off to England, to fogs, etc., but not for long—I only have one concert at Bournemouth on March 2nd, then Berlin with the Philharmonic on March 10th & 14th. Then ten days breathing space in Florence—well, perhaps three chamber music concerts, but that is just fun; then fifteen concerts again in France and in Paris with Lamoureux on April 17th and 20th. "Im wunderschonen Monat Mai" I'll find myself in Florence, and I hope for the entire month, but one can never tell! Voilà, Mademoiselle! These are my dates if they interest you at all—I do not ask you to write for I know I do not deserve it, but in case . . . you see how highly I rate your kindness and generosity. . . . Always address me to 14 Lungarno Vespucci, Florence. Mother forwards on my mail with splendid care. She writes wonders of the climate they are being blessed with—Oh! But there is only one Florence in the world!—you see I am incorrigible with my Italy.

Many letters more from Florence in the spring and from Monmouth Beach in the summer, and once again in the summer of 1910 there are exchanged visits at Oakdene and Florenzia; and the ecstatic, bookish friendship grows. In mid-October, after several postponements, he sails on the *Kronprinzessin Cecilie* and writes to Mary:

It will be a delight to bask with Henry James—Thank you, thank you and thank you—you're a trump to have sent the books—But now about Italy—and your visit. You'll be able, will you not? remember Mother wants you singly or in a group—just so that you come. . . . Can it be possible that only six weeks ago found me enjoying nectorial tranquility in a Watteauesque fête champêtre in the sylvan glades of Oakdene? A fête champêtre of intimate friendship and art? Will May hold some of these for us in Florence? You are surely coming, are you not? Select your date before or after Christmas and come prepared to stay for months *and* months. *Tom Achelis is to be with us and it would be sport to organise some theatricals.*

By December of 1910, the Pyles have arrived in Europe and there is a barrage of letters from Albert, who is on tour, arranging the forth-

Albert Spalding and André Benoist, early in their collaboration of nearly forty years.

coming visit to Florence and possibly a meeting sooner, in Munich, where Scott is pursuing his art studies and Albert has concert engagements. From Leipzig, he writes:

How good you are to me! If you could see the way I prize those two folios inscribed with your unmistakable, almost Japanese, characters! Most of all, the one which came to-day and announced the joyous certainty *of your coming to Florence. And to meet in Munich! Think of it! In less than a week! In half-an-hour I play a debut in Leipsic,* c'est dur*! Imagine that all the musical pedagogues are to be present—Nikisch, Reger, Hans Litt—in fact a long list of mighty and terrifying names. Reger is perfectly charming, I've come to know him so well during those last days spending many hours at his house playing his music notably the Sonata without accompanist—do you remember it? I played it out under the trees that famous day of ours—This Sonata is the magnet that brings him to the concert tonight. . . . This morning I returned to his house to read his violin concerto (very long but exceedingly beautiful) which he insists on my learning—enfin telling me a thousand head-turning things which do not bear repeating. But I know you would be interested and pleased at my good fortune. I'll tell it in Munich in detail, if you would like!*

The Pyles' visit to Florence came off famously and the rest of the winter of 1911 his letters to Mary were full of reminiscences of shared delights in Florence and Tuscany—and at the height of the social season, there were many brilliant occasions to recall. Then letters in late February and March, and the hope that she may be in Florence again for his March 27 concert. It is also a time of intensive composing for Albert under the tutelage of Antonio Scontrino, the foremost master of composition of the day. Albert urges Mary to come in March because in April he must be off to England for extensive touring there during the brilliant coronation year. His accompanist there is to be Coenraad V. Bos.

There is a short break in the letters during the summer of 1911. The Pyles were abroad, and it was Albert's first full summer of intensive music rehearsal with André Benoist, who would accompany him on his fall and winter European tour.

The first tangible evidence that his father had fully accepted Albert's chosen career was his engagement of André Benoist as his son's permanent accompanist. Benoist was the most acclaimed accompanist of the great singers and instrumentalists then performing in America. R. E. Johnston, a leading music manager in New York, had introduced him to Albert two years before. Professionally and personally, the two were in total accord from the very beginning of what became a lifelong companionship and collaboration with only two breaks, during World War I and World War II. Spalding volunteered for service in the Italian campaigns in both wars.

A letter to Mary in late October of 1911 clearly indicates how his career has developed.

I know you will be interested to hear of my concert at Carnegie Hall on Saturday. . . . I have never felt more "keen" on playing and the result satisfied me more than I could have hoped. . . . The Reger Sonata was listened to with great interest for at present his name together with Sir Edward Elgar's is being discussed in musical circles more than any other. . . . His sonata seemed to speak very strongly to the hearts of all the people present for there was a burst of applause at the close of the fugue. Some of the critics quibble at it a little but for the most part are keen, and for my playing the praise from the press has been unanimous—even my old enemy Krehbiel of the Tribune *says only fine things tho' the article is so short—due to the fact that* he only came to the concert before the very last number—*and this is the attention that the (supposed) dean of our critics pays to the first production in New York of an important new work—but let that pass!. . . I am now putting my hopes on your being here in December when I appear with the Thomas orchestra producing the Elgar concerto in this country for the first time. There will be a storm of comment over this work, also, for Elgar, too, has many enemies—in fact all the great ones have. But it has such a deep note of beauty—I have grown to love it as well as any modern work. It is broad and impressive like the Brahms, perhaps a trifle more sombre but of that school. Stock agrees with me that it is the finest since Brahms and this opinion from the great Conductor pleased me immensely for the work has been so "slammed." I am playing all over the globe between now and December—going as far south as St. Louis and New Orleans and as far west as Lincoln, Nebraska. . . . Then I have my concerts with the Thomas orchestra in Chicago, in Philadelphia and in Boston, winding up in New York and Brooklyn on December 13th, also intervening dates in Buffalo, Newark, Plain-*

field and (don't be shocked) a Sunday night at the New York Hippodrome. This is not as bad as it sounds for they are giving beautiful concerts there — the evening I play, the Russian Symphony Orchestra, Alice Nielson, and Rosa Ohtaska, all take part.

Whether before or after that Hippodrome date we cannot be sure, but it is certain that they declared their love and he proposed marriage at about this time. Both families reacted with the strongest disapproval. Mrs. Pyle was most dubious about her daughter sharing the uncertain fortunes of a concert violinist and the peripatetic life-style of a touring artist; Albert's mother and father were adamant about his need for more time to build his career without the distraction and added responsibility of a beautiful young wife. Furthermore, Marie Spalding was neither ready nor willing to give up her guardianship of his career.

The concert seasons of 1911-1912 and 1912-1913 were extremely busy ones. Before his extensive European tours, Mrs. Pyle apparently spoke to him about his and Mary's continuing voluminous correspondence. There is an allusion to this in his letter written in St. Petersburg in early March of 1913:

Alors et alors et alors — you write me something in your last letter about your mother's changed attitude, etc., etc. — that she does not consider the present situation fair to you — that she was right on the point of writing to me. Listen, my dear girl! In that famous conversation which I had with your mother before I left New York she exacted the promises (que vous savez bien!) in such an earnest way from me to rest on the present neutral ground for at least a year "else I should never give my consent to Mary's marrying you — and I know she would never marry without my consent!" that I have my word of honor to act as I have tried to act (but O! — if you knew how difficult it has been!) — and I am not afraid that you misunderstand me — nor have lost faith in my power to succeed. Success is coming very fast indeed but like everything else one must have a little patience.

Following the several seasons of extensive touring, the mounting successes, the exhilaration of recounting his adventures, and the joy of receiving her appreciative answers, there came a time when they decided to free one another and put their relationship to the test. Years later, Mary said this total release in a prolonged courtship was the greatest proof of its true sincerity. She liked to recommend it to impatient young lovers. So for more than three years they neither saw each other nor wrote, even exchanging greetings only through relatives and friends.

At the close of the spring season of 1914, Albert had played some fifty or sixty engagements throughout Europe and a series of recitals in Egypt. A contract had been signed to tour South America in the summer of 1915. By August Germany had declared war on Russia, then France, and a few days later Great Britain, too, was at war. Two and a half years went by and then American lives were lost when the *Lusitania* was sunk. America was shocked, but returned Woodrow Wilson to the presidency on the slogan: "He kept us out of war." A few weeks after his inauguration, the United States went to war.

In the meantime, because of the war in Europe, Albert had been playing almost continuously throughout the United States. He got to know his own country as he had not known it before, he said, and it was an experience that in those troubled days demanded answers within oneself. He was troubled by the widespread indifference to the issues of the war and the assumption that America's economic power carried no obligation or responsibility beyond enjoyment. When the declaration of war finally came, he felt released from his inner struggle and immediately sought how he could serve his country. The remainder of the season's concerts were played with frequent trips to Washington to seek a commission. His fluency in French, Italian, and German and his disciplined self-reliance were recognized assets. Much of the summer was spent awaiting orders but happily in the company of Jacques Thibaud and Pierre Monteux and their wives, who were all in residence at Monmouth Beach.

When word finally came, he wrote immediately to Mary asking if she would see him. "Time, distance, and separation found me unchanged. But to Mary it might perhaps have meant the end of our relationship. The way to find out was to write," he says in *Rise to Follow*. Mary answered promptly, they met, he proposed again – she didn't say "yes" but she didn't say "no." They agreed to resume their correspondence.

The letters started immediately and from their tone it is clear that the ecstatic friendship had intensified. He sailed for Paris on the

Carmania, writing from shipboard on the 20th of September and on the 30th after it landed. Thereafter they wrote as often as possible until the war ended, he was demobilized, and they were reunited – a heart-rending struggle. His letters of 1917 and 1918, compelling in spite of censorship, are truly love letters to his beloved Mary. From 1919 on, he invariably closes with "Ton Albert qui t'adore," and this became his signature to her in the daily letters of his lifetime.

Rhapsody
assai rubato

Thursday, 2 January 1919

My dearly Beloved: Three letters this morning, che festa! And—and—and your Xmas cable came—such a thrill it gives one to have a direct message—even a delayed cable seems like a dear caress from my own Mary—the thought of our near (do you hear it, *near*?) meeting—our work practically finished—a few loose threads will be cleared up in a few days. Then our orders are to proceed to France and we will be sent home by first available means.

Tomorrow the President arrives and [there are] great and festive doings. We are all to be on duty at the station when the train pulls in—and then there will be a reception tomorrow evening at the Campodoglio—a memorable occasion—really a historic event.

Spent yesterday quietly—composing most of the day—have nearly completed last movement of Sonate—this while the first two are still hanging on the branch—half [ripe].

My darling—I understand perfectly how trying my letters must seem—so indefinite, so vague as to plans. You realize that I was sensing what would happen and its consequences to us. Don't call me cautious! Lord knows! I am a seething, boiling cauldron—you'll be scared I'm so violent and rash in my temperament. Can't you see my pen shaking and there are the imprints of my teeth on the bedpost every night! If you dare mention that I am not eager—I'll punish you by kissing you a million times to stop your blasphemy! You are the Queen of my heart and soul—you know it so thoroughly you can afford to jest—Enfin! I love you for it—you delicious whimsical being—Eloisine as Diane of the Crossways (I always think of Meredith's heroine in connection with you). Do you know I brought Meredith's letters with me from Florence (your gift)—and joy to touch a book your hand has touched. Love me, my own dear sweet, love me as much as you can—I need your tenderness and your love—this absence has been rich only with thought of you. *Ton Albert qui t'adore.*

Albert in his World War I uniform.

Sunday, 5 January 1919

Dearest Mary – The reception at Campodoglio was wonderful – only in Rome could such a thing be given – my vantage point right by the statue of Innocent III. Immediately before the statue on a raised dais were the four gold armchairs for the royal and presidential personages. At a little after ten there was a fanfare of trumpets to announce their arrival – the Queen entered on Mr. Wilson's arm, followed by the King and Mrs. Wilson. The rest of gilded royalty came on – Duchess of Aosta, Prince of Udine, Duke of Genoa, etc. – also General Diaz and Mrs. Diaz (pleased to have a smile of recognition from the General – had not seen him since April). A fine speech from Prince Colonna, Mayor of Rome, conferring on the President the honorary citizenship of Florence [*sic:* Rome], and a handsome present to Mrs. Wilson in the shape of a gold replica of the Roman Wolf. Mr. Wilson replied with a very grateful speech in which his excellent knowledge of history stood him in good stead. He spoke, of course, in English but many people there could understand and it aroused much enthusiasm. Does it interest you to hear that Mrs. Wilson looked well, dressed in blue satin with plenty of tulle to soften? The Queen in white and very stately – she walks well – she wore the famous tiara of brilliants surmounted with pearls as big as plover's eggs. How fortunate for the Savoy family to have her virile, healthy Montenegri blood. The result shows in the children.

Have made two songs for you – completed both of them to the words you sent me – No. 1 – "When June is come" – should suit your voice. Workmanship not bad and develops quite spontaneously and is, I think, suited to the words. No. 2 – "In a fountain court" – had a quite different and much freer treatment. This I think is très réussie. It took me some time to find just the sort of acquative tonality, peace and quiet to picture the "peace of June" in a fountain court. I have a G flat insistently repeating that is good fun to image as anything you like. A thousand tender greetings, my dearest love, and my heart has tried to say to you via song what letters cannot – *Toujours ton Albert – qui t'adore.*

Wednesday, 8 January 1919

Carissima Maria mia – A delicious letter from you from Atlantic City. How fine you should have had that little jaunt with your dear mother. Your charming picture of the sea – how you love it! – brought *it* and *you* to me so closely. Am playing in Bologna Saturday and Sunday – to donate my fee to Italian Red Cross and the Major [Glendenning] is giving a like sum along with mine (1000 lire). It is for the Quartetto Society in the Old Liceo Hall where I took my diploma in 1903. Luba [d'Alexandrowska] will play with me. We are doing Franck Sonate, my Suite, a Beethoven Sonate and Lekeu Sonate. Then on Monday I'm playing here in Rome for the Duchessa Sermonetta (Vittoria Colonna) of Charity I Mutilatti. Old Tetrazzini will sing and Franchetti will play my accompaniments. Saw Tito Ricordi yesterday and am lunching with him today. He's down here for the new Puccini operas. Were they a success in N.Y.? The man certainly does understand the theatrical popularity business and at least in Bohème did an excellent piece of lyric writing. Toscanini comes to Rome Sunday. Hope to see him. He is certainly an extraordinary figure. I have a hunch qu'il a [grande envie] d'être Senateur – still pretty young for it. Believe that Marconi was only one made under 42.

What a shock Col. Roosevelt's death! Our flag at half mast, of course. A great American and a great patriot – I have a real sense of personal loss. Spanish fever again rampant – It's really quite serious though I do discount some of the hysteria that always accompanies such plagues. The Italian government has decorated me with the Cross of the Crown of Italy – a very nice decoration. Have not yet received the official document or insignia – Tacoli informed me it would come today or tomorrow. I was really quite pleased as it came in recognition of personal services – and not a diplomatic courtesy. The Gods are witness that I've done little or nothing to deserve it, but it's a bright-colored little ribbon (red & white) to wear and I am happy if it will please you.

Thursday, 9 January 1919

Dearest Mary: Had very interesting afternoon yesterday. Called on Toscanini. He received me most cordially – said he had such a nostalgia for New York but could not get on with the powers of the Met. Told me all his woes. He promised to come some evening next week to hear my compositions. Then I had a call on Maury (the Deputy) – you know, he is a great personal friend of General Diaz – and it's through him that I met the General together with LaGuardia. Maury had written a long letter to LaGuardia on the Dalmation situation which he wanted to read to me. Very interesting and I think probably LaGuardia may read it in the House. Maury is trying to arrange another meeting for me with the General for this afternoon – at the Diaz home. I would greatly enjoy this. He has promised me one of the General's pictures – am not an autograph seeker but such a personal souvenir from the hero of the Piave would be fine – especially as I knew him.

Bologna concerts are confirmed. Go on Friday night and return Rome Monday. I have three songs completed of the four you sent me – even a gay sprightly little tune for "Fanny's" charming verse [Fanny de Groot Hastings, poetess]. The best one is decidedly "In a Fountain Court" – I heard it for your voice. They are, of course, dedicated to you – but then everything is written for you, my Love. You are the Queen of my soul.

Friday, 10 January 1919

My darling: Off tonight for Bologna. Everything O.K. for concerts. (As I wrote you) it's with the Societa del Quartetto and takes place in the Liceo – fascinating historic place where I took my "violinist" diploma in 1903. This is the conservatory founded in the 18th Century by Padre Martini. Mozart studied there and took his diploma as a boy – in all Italy there is not a more interesting place musically. I am curious to see how my Suite will take. Our departure not yet fixed but it's bound to be soon now. You know I'm an optimist!!! My! how happy I'll be to send you that cable. We have been waiting so (it seems to me all our lives, toi et moi) and now this last stretch is almost intolerable.

Received yesterday the official letter from the Minister of Foreign Affairs Sonnino conferring on me the decoration of the Crown of Italy with title of "Chevalier" (Cavaliere), the medal is to follow. Of course, there are many Italians who have received this decoration, but I understand that it is quite a distinction for a foreigner.

Maury telephoned me yesterday. He is arranging a meeting with General Diaz. I got a lot of dope on his history and family – very interesting – Old Spanish family came to Naples end of the 18th Century with the Bourbon King Charles III. Is exceedingly simple with half a dozen titles but uses only his name Armand Diaz. Of course, he is adored here in Italy.

Have an excellent proposition from Wolfsohn's which I am inclined to accept. They are certainly the best agency in the country, and the only one I would consider going with. It's a guarantee they'll give and a good one.

Will write you from Bologna. Were you ever there? Together with Padova, the seat of Italian learning and medicine. Luba greatly excited over the concerts – an excellent appearance for her, she has never played in Bologna, and I am glad she should have it. She may remain in Florence on her way back. Luba is in many ways a strange mixture, but au fond a fine woman and has developed splendidly as an artist. She does the Franck and Lekeu Sonates as well as you could wish. I am playing, of course, on my Hill "trench violin" – but it gives good results. Maybe its bright red varnish will swear a little at the old portraits in the Liceo hall, ma pazienza. I have such a nostalgia to touch my Guarnerius.

Thursday, 14 January 1919

Such a festa on my return to Rome! Five letters – and this morning another one. Almost feel as tho' I had had a talk with you a viva voce. You are an angel to write so often and – O my dear! how touched I was that you should have sent flowers to my mother – you quite spoil me with your beautiful and generous praise, my really best merit is in loving you devotedly.

The concerts in Bologna were a great success and also the one in Rome [a benefit for the children's fund]. . . . All Rome there including members of the Royal family – H.R.H. Duchess of Aosta and Princess Jolanda. It was really a good and successful charity – and a personal satisfaction to me as evidence that I am fit for public playing.

A little delay in some records has put off our departure for a few days. How beautifully you express yourself, dearest – but I won't listen to your "fausse modestie" – your letters are part of *you*, as you really are, and as I love you – that gives them their rare quality for me. The military cape I will get for you if it is possible. Only they are not grey – but blue! – a greyish blue. It should be becoming to you but then what is not – you are so lovely a creature.

Had dinner with the Major last night. He said definitely that we

Captain Fiorello LaGuardia and his adjutant Lieutenant Albert Spalding.

should be off in a week or so – heartening news – if only we could fly home. What you will be feeling I can't imagine, and don't dare hope it is half what my sensations are. Do you wonder at my incoherence. Yes, my dear, the songs are yours, and for you only – I am even jealous not to have them published – I would like you – only you – to sing them – dearest, sweetest. There is a phrase which really expresses a thought and throb of my heart to yours in the Arthur Symons – the last line – and I dreamed of it all night long. As I am coming so soon, will not send them – do not trust the mails.

Of course, my love, we shall have ourselves to ourselves, for a time at least – and we'll go anywhere that fancy and your wish can lead us. Let it not be too definite or planned. It would be so delicious and restful to give way for once in a lifetime to every whim of the moment, n'est-ce pas?

Had a long talk with Carlotti [Italian entrepreneur] in Bologna. He has desires for a Spain tour and I gave him this field – but not for the near future. This summer must be completely free. Next winter 1919-1920 I have to play the States and get those blessed contracts off my chest, but 1920-21 we could dream for a while in Spain, Italy and Egypt – with a few – not too many concerts. Would that please you? And on the way back from Egypt perhaps Constantinople, Bucharest and the Balkans. Only we'll take it easily – tu sais que je n'ai pas la folie des grandeurs – and do not want to play too often. We have our lives to live – and now that my affairs seem to be shaping themselves more than comfortably we can breathe easily and now and then live some lazy long days with only our love to occupy us – no preoccupation over a missed concert or two. Don't berate me as too impractical – you'll see how well it will work out. *Love – and ever more love – Your own Albert.*

Wednesday, 15 January 1919

Dearest and ever dearest – Monday – perhaps – Tuesday probably – but next week surely – can it really be that it means we are off? A thousand winged thoughts and each a tender one are crowding the wireless lines to my Beloved. My heart! It thumps like an Italian locomotive (tu dois le reconnaître).

Your cape is ordered. It will be ready Friday (promised!). It is the nicest blue I could find, with a silver grey sheen – excellent quality and nearly, if not quite, waterproof. But let us not speak of commissions – you know what a joy it is to do this. Don't deprive me of it! If you knew the happiness to have some such little service to do for my "deare ladye Faire." Busy packing, but a sympathetic "corvée" when one thinks all it implies.

Rome is a trifle colder – sun always – but your love the brightest and most warming sun of all.

Thursday, 16 January 1919

Three adorable letters – what more can I say that you do not already know? That you are you – that is the wonder of the world for me. What a hectic time for you – and your lunch with LaGuardia – How dared he "look you over"? I don't forgive him that, but of course he loved you at sight. But what a gossip! – and what was it he said of his connection with Luba? Don't believe it – the sly dog was trying to draw you out. Confound him – mais qu'est-ce qu'il a dit donc? Enfin we'll have a grand pow-wow when I'm home, dearest, and praise be to the All Highest entre toi et moi jamais le besoin d'une arrièrepensée.

How could LaGuardia ever get the impression I was careful and orderly – tutt' altro! And so you liked his fair Thea? Understand she has a fiery temperament and more than once makes Fiorello tremble.

As to you, dearest, your tenderness is the most priceless jewel of a thousand years.

To Florence on Saturday eve. Have to have your package from Stella Traverso – and embêtements à propos Buitraga's violins – they must be sent home. He willed them to a certain Mrs. Wait who now commences to make trouble. Have not sent them before on account of the impossibility of shipments – war risk, etc.

Friday, 17 January 1919

My dearest – Such a wealth of correspondence – after the festa yesterday – two more letters this morning – and such letters – the flood gates of Heaven are open and I am bathed in unalloyed happiness.

Mme E. [Esterle] left Rome yesterday. She left me a present – a marriage souvenir – and a Royal one it is. Imagine my delight that it is "Directoire" – a small gilt urn for oil or incense burning, classic in design and quite unique. A museum piece – I'm sure you'll love it. She left it with a few words asking me to convey "à la gentille personne qui sera votre compagnon dans la vie," the expression of her best wishes, adding that she hopes to have the privilege of meeting you some day. Think I had already written you that she is the widow of Senator Esterle, one of the most prominent Italian industrialists and patriots. What a pity that he died before the revindication of his native Trento.

My dear, in regard to the Italian Jugo Slav Question, I have volumes to tell you. It is a most complex situation and I don't pretend to understand it thoroughly, but have several angles. Confess to an Italian leaning, but much to be said in both ways.

Yes! Cyril Maude is delicious, n'est-ce pas – and it is *real humor* – not "horse play" – as you say. Heard the three new Puccini operas last night and enjoyed them in spite of myself. Tabarro really has pages of Puccini at his best – and Gianni Schichi one loves if only for lines about Florence – and the delicious costumes.

Irrepressible LaGuardia—of course, he'd tell the "Bobo" story, he loves it—and it's quite true that it loses nothing in the telling. Indignantly deny, however, the gurgling of soup in the King's face!!! Fiorello trying to shock you. I do confess to having thoroughly enjoyed my dinner—court etiquette did not affect my appetite.

Molinari and the Blumenstiels came yesterday to hear some of my compositions—new ones. Also played some unaccompanied Bach—they couldn't believe that it was a trench violin—perhaps a uniform covers a multitude of sins. But my playing, sérieusement, is really good—no trace of a year and more inactivity. Yes, dearest, it may be possible—your plan—should we go to Italy for spring and early summer (maybe a trip to Spain if you'd like it!) but of course no answer possible to this letter. Think I may be sailing almost with it. What a wonderful world it is—my heart to yours in the tenderest kiss.

Monday, 27 January 1919
from Paris

The long cable I have just sent you must have astonished my dearest as much as the necessity to send it astonished me. Ten days since last writing you and I thought to have sailed by now. Let one begin at the beginning. First, a cable from Boardman stating that Adjutant General's office had ruled possible a discharge on this side. Of course, you heard of this from my people. However, with my plans all made to come home, I can't deny that it was a disappointment to make others. Anyway, I wired Chief of Air Service quoting Boardman's information and his reply confirmed this on Friday of last week (just as I was leaving Rome). As cables take so infernally long from Italy—no object to cable till reaching Paris—last night. Then, too, on reaching here certain misgivings as to being sent home promptly arose even though every indication leads me to hope for a quick discharge. How does this affect you, my dearest? My only consolation is from a delicately expressed wish on your part to come over, but O, I *am* disappointed for the moment and can't help saying so. To have you in my arms is about the only remedy I can think of. Don't know if this letter will reach you before you sail, but shall continue to write now till I hear from you. If only they don't start me at a desk job again!

Your batch of dear letters greeted me here, what a provident angel, I was speechless with happiness when I found them. You *have got* a head on your shoulders. Yes, my dearest, from one standpoint this is better and quieter all around. A simple wedding and we can dream some golden days among the hill towns and on the lakes. If Venice is possible – there, too and, who knows, perhaps Spain. I do not expect to play, or at least not often. Can we be married as soon as you come over – what will I not ask – and keep on asking? I have so much to say to you that will not, *cannot* be written, but it is all in harmony and accord with what you will want and desire, this I feel!

All in all, I am reconciled to Europe though burning up at the thought of a possible delay in your sailing. Come soon, dear love –

Wednesday, 29 January 1919

Dearest Mary – I don't suppose I can hope for a cable before next week but you can imagine, of course, how I am on pins and needles to hear. My application has gone in and I am given good reason to hope for quick action. Have quite a feeling of nostalgia when I think of my lost trip to America, but after all this may work out for the best. I do hope you are going to have a comfortable trip over. Will meet you in Genoa or Naples whichever you prefer. Paris is very gay, but none so pretty as my Mary. Of course, you shall have your gloves, my sweet – and your mother, too.

I am not writing you a word of politics, tho I am thick in them, for the simple reason that I must see you and tell you some things. Confess that I am nearly heartsick over situation. The pitiful spectacle of this petty squabbling is something to disgust one from politics for life. I can give you "des tuyaux" of that, rest assured. I dread to think of your disillusionment. One's ideals do suffer a shock!!!

After all, it doesn't matter – you are you – et ça me suffit – Je t' embrasse tendrement –

Wednesday, 29 January 1919

Ma bien chère amie – Your good letter of January 2nd just at hand. How exciting that you should think of coming – you and your mother. I know your splendid spirit too well to suppose that any pleadings or warnings of danger would be of any avail, but O my dear do be careful – and, if possible, come by a French boat. It seems to me that they are the most spared and the route to Bordeaux the best. After once located in Paris, I think you would not have great difficulty in finding an attractive apartment in a quiet but fairly central quarter, say the Parc Monceaux arrondisement. The chief trouble about an apartment is the chauffage central (coal, etc.), but with spring coming on, one could be bolder than in October.

30 January

No chance to continue. A batch of work burst in upon me and I have been constantly on the run ever since. Last evening the French General commanding the [illegible] Army Corps in the Provincia of [illegible] gave to the American officers stationed at Headquarters L. of C. a magnificent fête in the Hôtel de Ville and it was most impressive. Our own general made a splendid impression with a well-worded speech in French on our absolute determination to see justice done not only to Belgium but to France also – in the matter of Alsace-Lorraine. Can you imagine the enthusiasm?

Jan. 31 – Friday

Et voilà! This letter goes by fits and starts – mostly fits, I think. Will try and wind it up now so that it can go out by today's mail. The weather continues mild – almost springlike – and the sun is almost as frequent and as friendly as in Florence. I wonder when we shall ever see Florence again. Peace seems yet a long way off and it *must not be even wished for* until this business is properly and ultimately settled.

Thursday, 31 January 1919

Dearest Mary – Every day to Rue Tronchet [Paris office, A. G. Spalding & Bros.] but still not an answer. I cannot help a certain uneasiness about it all. It's dreadful this separation of thousands of miles – please God – we'll never be separated so again. And then, too, about your passport. Of course, you can obtain one – or you'd never have written as you did. Still I do hear how difficult they make it – and all these things make me uneasy. On that score, am expecting almost immediate action on my application – but have I been wise to put it in? Enfin, no use worrying. The war is over – and we have each other. The details are annoying, but – no! – I confess my stock of patience is all gone – no amount of philosophising does me any good. It's your dear eyes I want to look into mine and to read in them all that my heart is saying. I am wondering what boat you will be sailing on and if your mother comes with you. After all it's partly her suggestion which decided me, too, and now I am quite reconciled that it's going to be O.K. and for the best – a quiet marriage here and we can steal away to some hill towns and a perfect Nirvana to everything but ourselves. But O! for that reassuring cable – when will it come? Major G. still in Paris. His orders not even yet requested. They are piling on more Italian work and, of course, I come in for my share. Don't know when they'll get away. No more mail from you since the Good Samaritaine bunch I found on arrival here. Enfin, I have my thumbs crossed.

Tuesday, 4 February 1919
from Hotel Continental, Paris, to 375 Park Ave.

I must think quietly for a moment not to yell! My own blinding disappointment is swallowed up, for the moment, in the realization of the pain which I read between the lines of your cable just received. Beloved, my dear Beloved, how can this cruel thing have happened? I am trying to reconstitute the entire series of events. Can find no answer to it, but the impossibility of communicating properly at a distance of 4100 miles. Then, too, my own hasty action in putting in application here. But this, dearest I had to do – decide one way or other, for the alternative meant probability of my being grabbed for a job here in France for some months to come. True LaGuardia's request came in, but a certain amount of pressure and request for my services would have hampered this. Surely, O surely, he can get you a passport. Have just sent you a cable as follows: "Have cabled LaGuardia requesting he take action obtain your passport; make every effort sail and wire me results; my plans made believing you could come. If this proves impossible will await arrival Italy my parents and after short visit with them will sail home." But this is a dismal alternative, as it means delaying our meeting till April or May. Of course, I will not allow anything to stand in way of sailing then if I have to move Heaven & Earth and charter a boat. I'll get home somehow.

But the bitter disappointment of it all. Of course, I thoroughly understand Mother's strong desire to come over after five years' absence from Florence & shall not allow a word of criticism to mar her pleasure in so doing. But I have had some misgivings all along as to this and feel that I have been working in the dark as to the real situation. Now answer me, dearest, frankly—is it that you would rather *not* come even if you could obtain a passport? and have I misinterpreted the spirit of your letters? No! That's not possible. It may be unreasonable to feel as I do and, of course, in the sudden ending of the war when we had every prospect of years, waiting these several weeks or months appear as nothing—and yet, I can't help it, I am bitterly rebellious, and feel like biting something when I think of your disappointment through it all. Your generous self-abnegation in telling me to do as I think best does not disguise in the least to me your pain. More than your actual disappointment you feel—you cannot help but feel—that I have acted hastily and with an apparent disregard to your desires—Mary, is this true? O to put my arms around you, you mustn't, mustn't believe it. I had to act—and act quickly—and now my only consolation would be to have the conviction that your own disappointment was tempered by an absolute belief in me and my love, my all-embracing love of you. I could almost bear the further separation of a few more weeks with a light heart if I had this conviction. Tell me that it's true, Mary, if you don't want me to lose the few wits that remain. Will write again tomorrow, I hope in a saner way. This today is one long howl of distress. *Yours for life—Albert—*

Wednesday, 5 February 1919
from Hotel Continental to 375 Park Ave.

I can write more rationally today, Beloved. It was an unpardonable letter I sent you yesterday in the first bitterness of disappointment. Your second cable has just come to which I have sent an answer. How like you, my dear, in your generous unselfish way to urge only consideration of Italian propositions, but how little you can judge the real motives of my action if you could suppose that I would accept your sacrifice (and mine) for such a reason. The professional reasons could all go "plum to the Devil"—the reasons I took action as I did can be summarized as follows:

1. Mother's strong desire to come over to Italy. Many questions about the house & property to set right.

2. My belief that you could and would come over and a quiet

wedding in Florence seemed to your liking and also supported by your mother's suggestions.

3. The necessity for an immediate separation from the service and the possibility of this held out as against the offer of a captaincy and more months of service.

4. (And this one of the most important and above all do not breathe of it to LaGuardia –) I have every reason to suspect a Congressional investigation and a strong desire on part of LaGuardia to have me return for this and a contrary desire on my part not to be party to it. Cannot write you any details, but I know that you will realize without me telling you how distasteful (and useless) to me such a proceeding would be. I could not escape it if I returned as a soldier. I have only intuition (but it's a strong one) that tells me this.

I have no need to tell you what a friend I consider LaGuardia and how much I admire him in certain ways, but I sometimes question his judgment and his impetuosity, and for that reason I know that I am doing a wise thing in grasping my liberty as a civilian while I can. Can you read between the lines and understand many things which discretion prevents my writing. If you should see LaGuardia be extremely guarded not to let the shadow of such a thought enter his mind. My application was approved and orders issued today sending me to St. Aignan for discharge – this means that I am probably a civilian in another week's time.

Dearest, I can not tell you what I felt on receiving your second cable – Not that it lessened the disappointment one jot of our mutual sacrifice, but the further evidence of your beautiful, generous, self-abnegation and above all your confidence in me and my love was a dear tonic to me. You are unique in meeting with such a spirit a situation which only your courage and unselfishness could stimulate me to face –

Am still in hopes that you will be able to obtain a passport – and shall anxiously await a cable reporting on which action has been taken. But should this not prove the case then the plans outlined in my yesterday's cable and letter hold good – namely: that I will await arrival in Europe of Father and Mother, have a nice visit with them in Florence but shall of course make immediately arrangements to sail home in April or early May. Will see about this directly I arrive in Italy and will cable you results. In the meantime I will play a few important engagements in March in Italy, but not many. They all urge importance of this so strongly. I must say I can't see it, but still perhaps my vision is a bit colored. And now, my dearest, I must speak of something that I had meant only to touch upon when we met. In one of your letters you mentioned some gossip which Mrs. Loury had written your friend Margaret Sloane re Luba and myself. Your own treatment of the matter was so noble and dignified that I feel a certain hesitation in even mentioning it except that, if we are lovers, we are also comrades and so accept it in that spirit. Mrs. Loury deliberately misquoted what I said to her of Luba's playing. In that very "douce" manner she said some rather insipid things and asking my opinion I stated simply that I considered Luba "one of the greatest *women* pianists today" – I saw a great deal of Luba in Rome while she was staying with Mrs. Carpenter (Red X worker) in the same building – and Luba used the studio to practice in. All this I have written you. I have no fear that you will in the least misunderstand, and, indeed, know that you would approve the frank enjoyment of an honest friendship and musical interest – all the more spontaneously entered into because being deeply in love with someone else I felt that an arrière pensée could never arise. Luba is wayward and many times I am entirely out of patience with her lack of control, but I have a real affection for her – and with a clear conscience can affirm that I know it's in accord with what you would want me to be. If after a day of hard work it was my greater pleasure to spend an evening of music instead of a social engagement . . . have no doubt that my devotion to Beethoven & Schumann was attributed to something else. If you were less than *you* I could not write all this so frankly. I had rather have said, with your hand in mind and your eyes reading into my heart all that my pen can not say – But, Mary, my Beloved, I know that you do believe in me and that you believe me when I say that my life is an open book whose pages I am willing and anxious to have your pure beautiful hands turn. There is not a chapter but which is dedicated to devoted and cherishing love of you. Tell me that you feel this to be true or have I tired you out?

Now as to prospects. Doubtless you have heard from my people that the Wolfsohn contract is signed and a very good guarantee. We will not be as rich as Croesus but at least it is very comfortable and my own private income and the Edison royalties should permit me to count on a budget of $10,000 or $12,000 a year with ample to lay aside over and above. I have stated conservatively as the net income should be quite double that, mais il est toujours prudent de compter en petit, n'est-ce pas? Our wedding in June and our summer to ourselves, I feel my yesterday's letter to have been wicked in view of so much happiness in store for us — Dearest, your love is the precious gift straight from Heaven — and your cable and expression of faith in me has started a chorus singing Hallelujah again —

Friday, 7 February 1919
from Hotel Continental to 375 Park Ave.

My darling: Perhaps I am a hopeless optimist — but I can not get over the feeling that another day or two will bring me a cable announcing the obtaining of your passport and that you — and perhaps your mother also are sailing. Glendenning will probably release me Monday or Tuesday (today is Friday!) will go to St. Aignan then — a question of a day or hours before my discharge is fully effected.

I do hope both my cables went through O. K. and that they explained to you a measure of what I have been feeling — My letters are such incoherent "hodgepodges" that I don't wonder if you hold up your hands in despair.

Other than your gloves, I found two delectable scarfs — or veils (can be used as either) — quite original — at Charvet's that I couldn't resist — they need your head & shoulders to set them off — really a delicious yellow, the one — and the other your favorite green. You'll look more than ever like a delicious wood nymph. Must tell you rather a sweet present and a card from Stella Traverso — enclosed a card to you and a charming table piece of filet and embroidery — she remembers you from Monmouth Beach as a little girl — and — well! You will find her card very charming I think. Other than the Florentine souvenir she gave me a generous check with request that we select something. This we can do jointly — quoi? You would be greatly amused at sight of my small Army locker — its contents are almost compromising!!!!! I am in hopes of obtaining permission to travel back to Italy in uniform as it will facilitate baggage. It's a negative consolation to disappointment, but still something to tell you that Major G. is still retained here and no immediate prospect of a release to America. My road would, of course, have been the same. It *will* be a relief to get out of the service after nearly 18 months and, at most, it means only a two month's delay.

Sunday, 9 February 1919
from Hotel Continental to 375 Park Ave.

Perhaps I am foolish, but I can not help having the feeling that somehow you can and will obtain a passport. It does seem that a direct application to Washington, for purpose of marriage – your fiancé's residence Florence, Italy – and being impracticable for him to come over – for you to obtain it. This based, of course, on supposition that you want to come. The political situation seems to me more involved than ever. Have you a contact sufficient thru the newspapers to realize the direct clashing of interests? It's all a great pity and the result is of benefit only to our enemies. Germany, in spite of military defeat, and internal revolution, has an organisation and a discipline that we would be foolish to underrate – and they are ready to turn to their advantage every indication of indecision and dissension amongst us. The Major hopes now to have his orders to sail home by early March – qui sait? At all events you can not imagine what a relief for me to have my entire release from the service. I am really more tired that I like to admit – and am going to take a completely lazy rest. Shall go to St. Aignan Tuesday or Wednesday. There it is a question of a few hours, I understand. From now on send all your letters direct to Florence, 14 Lungarno Vespucci, am cabling you this as soon as discharge is actually effected. May leave for Florence by end of this week. Write me what you think, and if you are pleased over the Wolfsohn contract. One of its best features, to me it seems, is the lifting of all financial and mental responsibility of running a separate organization of my own. I am curious to learn too the results of this year's (6 months) Edison royalties. If as good as last year you shall have your emerald, and the nicest one I can find. You darling child, the happiness which the realization of your love and trust give me can never be expressed in stones, but a bit of green would look well on your beautiful hands – how dare you call your hands large? – those sensitive beautifully shaped hands! I am hungry for the warmth of their clasp in mine this very moment.

Tuesday, 11 February 1919
from Hotel Continental to 375 Park Ave.

I am still waiting for answers to my cables to you and to LaGuardia. In meantime I am on a dead hunt around Paris for a little chap Edward

Brown whose mother heard he was dead but no news and it's like trying to find a needle in a haystock. My impression is the poor lad has gotten into trouble but is alive.

Yes, my dear, I have read *The Four Horsemen of the Apocalypse* and thoroughly enjoyed it. Almost the greatest novel of the war. Am still waiting for my release. Major still on pins and needles as to his fate. If I have a quick discharge I may go over to London for few days to visit Winthrop Rogers, the publisher. You remember them, n'est-ce pas? He has his own business now in London and it may be he will want to publish some of my new things which I would be glad to let him have. If only, if only you can come—and if you can't, I am coming to you—*soon*—*soon*—*soon*!!!

Wednesday, 12 February 1919
from HQ Am. Exped. Forces, Office of the Aeronautical Off.

Wrote you just a scratch of the pencil yesterday—this is a supplemental line. Am still on hot chase for information about Edward Brown. The d— — —d little fool has evidently been cutting up to beat the band. Every fresh trace of him discovers more unpaid bills, which I am trying to salt down so as they will not be presented to aggravate his already difficult position. I *am* distressed for his poor mother. She has already had so much trouble. No fresh news from you, either letter or cable, but a letter came in today from George Brown . . . urging me to stay over here and play a few concerts. He gave a few more details about the Wolfsohn contract, it seems they are bringing also a bit of pressure. Personally, I think it is all "bosh"—and I have already explained to you my real reasons for decision. O my darling! Our life must be, *will be*, one long tender dream. Did you have my letter mentioning tentative plans? I mean in regard to Spain & South America, etc., for 1920? Would this please you? Have a hunch it would, but you quite understand that I will never undertake anything without your pleasure and approval.

Friday, 14 February 1919
from HQ Am. Exped. Forces, Office of the Aeronautical Off.

Your cable just received—disappointed as I am I feel sure you have very real & excellent reasons for your decision. Perhaps your mother felt she couldn't sail and you not to leave her nor be married away from her—is it this? And if so, how out of patience with me you must be for my seemingly vaccilating policy, but no! My darling has given too many proofs of a wonderful understanding not to have appreciated my situation. Your two little words—"deepest love" give me that thrill and reassurance which I hunger for—I go to St. Aignan probably Sunday and hope it is only a question of hours there before complete demobilization. Italian papers have come and at last it looks as tho' the Major could get away and completely release me. All my property accounts are cleaned up in good shape—such a relief to have them off my shoulders. Countess de St. Maurice spoke of you today & asked "Is it true you are going to marry Miss Pyle?" and on my affirmative—added "I always knew you would—and am so pleased to know it. She has beauty, sense, dignity and great savoir faire"—I was as pleased as punch, you can well imagine, for she is a woman of quite keen judgment—and this was for me a further evidence of it. Finally found Edward Brown. Here in a military prison and has undergone a Court Martial—I am distressed at the thought of his poor mother. Wretched little scamp he was absent without leave for 32 days—pretty bad—altho' I am inclined to think they will not treat these cases as harshly now the war has finished.

No more mail, expect some letters to be coming now in a day or two. Everything indicated great satisfaction over my contract with Wolfsohn and perhaps it is just as well this is decided. It relieves my mind completely from all financial bother and worry. Also, Benoist writes that it will put a stop to the promiscuous announcements made by several different managements (some reliable & some not) that they had me—ce qui n'est pas chic!

Mother writes of your having some concert parties, etc. together—at Carolyn Beebe, Rudie Ganz—Ding Bust him! he never's programmed those pieces of mine—pazienza, Rudie was long on the words and is short on action! But presume he has his reason, the Rhapsody is absolutely new in form and treatment and may not prove successful. There is an entire misconception of the Italian situation here—and the friction caused by it is of profit only to the Germans. The two Latin races must realize that far more important than all strategical boundaries or frontiers is the racial and political and economic alliance—which will be their greatest safeguard against future aggressions—

Saturday, 15 February 1919
Hotel Continental

My darling: Your first letter (A) – has just come. I am heart-broken for the pain that I have caused you and your generous unselfishness and absolute loyalty does not in the least disguise this feeling. But how you do rise above things, O my dear one! And, of course, I understand your real reasons for not sailing and fully appreciate how your mother would feel not to be present at your marriage – our marriage – Do you not put me down as all kinds of a blockhead not to have foreseen all these things – and yet, my darling, in reading over your previous letters I think that you readily understand that my conclusions at the time were not based entirely on erroneous conceptions. But one thing in which your own intuition saves everything *was* and *is* that it is my decision. *Your* pleasure or your disappointment, my dear, is like a 1000 kiloweight against any such feathery considerations. How happy I am that you knew and felt this and in your tenderness wrote to console me with your trust and faith.

Tomorrow I go to St. Aignan. Return here Monday – will cable you then. Rome telegraphs asking for 2 concerts – one with orchestra at Augusteo and the other, a recital at Academy St. Cecilia. Have asked thousand lire each concert – don't know if they accept. They are to take place in March. I do not care to play in all more than 10 or 12 concerts. A good rest is what I need and intend to have. But I *need you* more than all that and immediately on arriving in Italy shall busy myself for booking passage home. Will cable you as soon as date is fixed. Will try and tentatively see about passage for my family, but doubt that they can obtain this, and I will not delay my sailing later than May. Sailings very difficult to book from Italy, but, of course, not so hard for a single man. O my dear, how I love you! You are simply adorable, that's all – and I hope never will be tired hearing me say it as an inevitable chorus you can't get away from.

Continued later – Am finishing these lines at office while waiting for a few papers. Viewed in perspective, I thoroughly understand and appreciate the wisdom of your decision – and if only I could drag the unhappy (brave but unhappy) strain, I should shout for relief and joy. I have been waiting so long – now eight years for the full consummation of a dream that 2 months more seems like nothing at all.

Haven't the faintest idea what I shall play in Rome, perhaps Poème

Portrait of Mary Vanderhoef Pyle painted by her brother Scott circa 1918.

of Chausson for one thing, if they can get the orchestrations. I have no orchestral stuff of my own here – or ready – tho' this is what had been requested. A very unpleasant corvée, this trip of mine tomorrow. All day in train, short distance, probably no place to sit down – enfin tous les conforts de chez soi!!! – but growling is never any use and it *will* be a relief to get one's final release.

Had a nice letter from good old faithful George Brown – tickled to death over the Wolfsohn contract though it means a discontinuance of his position with me. I am only hoping that Wolfsohn makes it worth his while to go with them. His qualities are all affirmative ones and loyalty to the core. And this is one of the things (*the thing*) that counts.

I know that it has been as hard as "pulling teeth" for the Major to get away from here. But it looks as tho' he would be able to leave next week for Brest and then it's a wild scramble for places on transports & ships going home. Going home! Hold yo' hosses, Sambo – Ah'll be goin' soon too! In the meantime my own true love, my arms are about you in one long tender embrace – My darling must never know a chagrin or the shadow of a disappointment – Your interests are mine & mine yours and nothing counts in the world except our Invincible Love – how true what you say – It's the all-conquering force – praise be! *Toujours ton Albert qui t'adore*

Tuesday, 18 February 1919
Hotel Continental

A civilian at last after two very muddy and, I must say, disagreeable days at St. Aignan. Now I am busy for Passport – Sauf-Conduite, etc., etc. On returning to Paris this morning found my Beloved's three letters B – C – D and supplemental E. Dearest, your heart-ache is mine and my arms with the tenderest love and devotion are about you – now this very moment. Where I do not, can not, *will not* follow my love is in her making issues out of circumstances. My heart and sympathy is entirely with you in realizing how you feel, but dearest, such issues *will never, can never* exist unless we allow the separation of three thousand miles of ocean and delayed means of communication to work its most deadly propaganda. I love you – you love me – we are soon to be one in human and spiritual love. These are things that really matter – you, who feel and think straight, must feel and believe them as I do. You will already have had my previous letters and in them

I gave you all the reasons, motives, impulses which prompted my sudden decision. My tenderness and distress urges me to repeat them – only discretion points out the fact that my Mary does not need the means of a Wagnerian Leit-motif to understand and grasp. This only I must say again frankly and squarely – and I know you believe it! No commercial or artistic reasons could have influenced me in the least, and never shall so far as you are concerned. Now, as to my "family and me, and you" – no, dearest, this is not an issue unless we choose to make it so. They will love and cherish you as the one woman who can make me happy – as I hope to deserve your mother's and Scott's love and faith by making you happy. You have been so closely, so beautifully united to your family that you can not fail to appreciate what it means as a guarantee for future happiness – but you also realize that these close family ties promote intense and even unreasonable feelings at times that if misinterpreted could be allowed to grow into vital issues. This must and will never happen between my Beloved and myself. Our love and our mutual happiness in each other shall be the spiritual guard against any such human frailties. I would not dare to write so frankly, dear, except to you, but you *do* understand. Now I ask you to understand something more. For the last year and a half my mother has been under an intense mental and physical (because mental!) strain. I know that never voluntarily would she, by an indifferent word or action cause you the slightest "chagrin" for she knows too well how this would be reflected tenfold in me. I know, too, of her deep admiration for you, and that her joy and pride in you will be complete with our happiness. You are too big and noble a woman to allow an issue to grow out of the natural fruits of this strain; and if you feel for a moment that you do not count with her – merely an incident – the next moment you will recognise that *this feeling is incidental* as are the causes which promoted it. It is perhaps true that one generation does not thoroughly understand the next one, but I do believe that it is the duty of our love, our faith in each other, our strength to bridge over, not widen any chasm. You are not "headstrong" nor "self-willed" as you believe that my parents think you, you dear generous-hearted, unselfish girl. But you have a quality of sensitiveness which (is adorable and I love you for it) sometimes plays havoc with you and how well I understand how this is aggravated by our cruel separation.

NEXT! You say "would it not have been better, kinder, if you had written me candidly about your feelings — as you did your family — or given your reasons in your cable so that I might not have been so completely in the dark on its receipt?" — This is a square, fair, and frank question and deserves the most explicit answer. In the first place, Mary dear, you are wrong in your statement that you "had written me you could not get over," and when I cabled I fully believed that you could, and would be glad to come. Second — all along my intense desire and intention was to come home and, indeed, having made exhaustive enquiries starting in November, of the Embassy and G.H.Q. the answers were always "that no provision had been made for the discharge of officers or troops in Europe" — This desire and intention to come home was absolutely sincere and would have been carried out in the face of the strong urgings to stay over — Mother's strong desire to come over, Father writing his intention to come in any event on account of the London business, Brown's cables and letters and your "neutral" attitude, even (as I thought) rather a leaning to come. The contras to all this for me were 1) the impossibility of discharge on this side, 2) my wish not to play at all this season (this partly overcome by success of Bologna concerts!), 3) difficulty of travel in Europe, 4) financial reasons which were more profitable for my return to States, 5) arrangements and plans for my next winter's season. Well! It all happened by suddenly — just before leaving Rome. Cable from Boardman stated decision of War Office to allow discharge in Europe and added that Wolfsohn contract had been signed. This disposed of Bologna concerts though you must believe that I have not the intention of playing but a very few times. About the same time I had some information which gave me the strong "hunch" of which I wrote you ten days ago — namely, the friction between LaGuardia and Glendenning and probability of Congressional investigation. Will not go all over this again but *please, please* keep it absolutely confidential, will explain in detail when I see you. I had first to verify in Paris truth of possibility of discharge and anyway this did not delay my cabling you or Mother as I was just about to leave Rome and cables go twice as quickly from Paris.

Takes 8 days to have a cable answered here — 15 or more in Italy. The best proof that I intended all along to come home was the fact of my not writing for a space of ten days — believed I was sailing — then, too, I was having a nasty time just then — physically. But I won't speak of this as it would be an entirely cowardly, inadequate, and unnecessary excuse to give. The action was hasty, certainly, and you had every justification and reason to feel hurt, surprised—and to doubt my good faith. The tenderness and sympathy in your dear pained letters does not blind me to this. But I had to decide and decide at once. In sum, my darling, the end of this long harangue is to beg you to believe in the only really vital issue—Our Love—and Our Happiness. All the rest are merely incidents, unless we make more out of them.

Sweetheart, our wedding will be in June and the summer ours all our very own—and all the rest of our lives, too. Do I read the signs wrong when I say that I can feel this very moment that you are thinking of me—understanding me—loving me? *Toujours Ton Albert qui t'adore—*

No more military titles—am a plain "civvy" now.

Thursday, 20 February 1919
Hotel Continental to 375 Park Ave.

Paris is a turmoil over dastardly attempt on Clemenceau's life—anarchy defeats its own ends by such senseless methods. Result is a greater Clemenceau popularity than ever before. Everyone is praying that the wound is not serious, but of course the physical shock alone for a man that age—still he has indomitable will and courage. It means so much for him to pull through. I suppose the excitement was very great in the States over the news. I will not be able to get away from Paris for several days. More passport difficulties than you can shake a stick at. Have to wire Rome Embassy for permission to issue one for Italy. I wired personally to the Ambassador requesting him to expedite it.

Rome has engaged me for the two concerts—one orchestral and one at the Accadèmia (recital) 16th and 21st March. Am playing Mendelssohn Concerto at the first one in Augusteo with orchestra. At second will play Corelli, Bach, Franck and some of my own things probably. Should be a musical audience and an interesting one.

Dearest, your counsels about resting shall be absolutely heeded. No one knows more than myself how it is needed and I shall take it willy-nilly!!! Now that there is no chance of needlessly worrying my darling, I will tell you that in addition to my other duties I did some flying—in fact, took an observer's license . . . at the School of Cento Celle and was about to be assigned to an Italian squadron when the war ended. It was intensely interesting—as I went through the entire course (under orders, of course, from Chef Aire Service!) including reconnaissance, wireless, photography, navigation, bombardment, machine gunnery, and was not a bad shot at that and came out with a very good flying record—maximum number of points. The wings which I shall never wear might look attractive on a hat of yours if you cared for them. Also have some interesting souvenirs in the shape of photos—a bully series of Rome—on day that Armistice was signed we took a big Caproni and flew low over the city—quite a sensation with all the people in the streets cheering. It is perhaps difficult to realize how absolutely essential one felt it for one's self-respect to get out of the non-combatant class of the army. Though I never had the satisfaction of dropping a bomb on a Hun, I could never have looked myself in the face if I had not made the effort and succeeded in doing more than merely desk work. LaGuardia opposed my application for flying always (with the best of motives) and was quite on the outs with me when I finally obtained permission to take the training from the C.A.S. I suppose you'll scold me roundly for never having written to you of this—and with reason, too, dearest, but for your special information (if you care for it) I kept a diary most of the time while flying—it wasn't for a long period—October and November—and I didn't have more than a total of 20 or 25 hours in the air. It will be an interesting souvenir to look back upon and the gold Italian observer's wing would look attractive on a little black toque for you. No, I haven't done a stroke of composing since I left Italy, but am copying out your songs which will send you from here. I think you'll like the Symons song—and perhaps—"When June is come" also will have a special significance for us both. Curiously enough both of the songs sing of June and I am superstitious enough to believe in symbols.

Saw a wonderful play last night by Sascha Guitry, played by a remarkable cast headed by Lucien Guitry, Sascha's father. Play, a narrative of episodes in Pasteur's life, all real characters. Original in form, strong in outline, sparkling dialogue. If you had only been with me how we would have thrilled together over it. I have a childish pleasure in good drama and joy to think that you have also—what good times we can have. Will you—and can you—enjoy quite a bit of travelling next winter? I don't mean any hard trips to out of the way places, but for the most part we can travel very comfortably and make a real honeymoon year—pleasure and work combined. There are loads of attractive places in the U.S. to visit and in spare days we can do delicious jaunts together.

Captain Fiorello LaGuardia with Caproni executive and plane, Foggia, 1918.

Sunday, 23 February 1919
Hotel Continental to 375 Park Ave.

Have not secured my passport yet, but hope to have it next week. Have a sleeper engaged for March 4th *sure* and a possibility of obtaining one sooner. Confirmatory cables just received of Father & Mother's sailing on the 27th due to arrive in Genoa about March 12th. I am going to make every effort to meet them there though it may be difficult with the acceptance of this Rome engagement. It looks as though it would be a very important concert. I am playing the Mendelssohn Concerto—and am busy practicing my scales and staccato. About the Rome notices which so disgusted you. They were in no sense criticisms—as it was a charity concert. I only sent them over as amusing little items. Lunched with Countess de St. Maurice today. She was most anxious to know your favorite color—Je ne peux m'imaginer qu'est-ce qui se prepare.

Paris is swarming with Americans. You can't turn the corner without running into legions of them, men & women. Had an amusing dinner last night with Hermann (Chief Pilot at Foggia). We dined at Henri's—he pleased as punch because of a commendation letter he had received from Gen. Patrick—Chief Air Service. I couldn't help smiling (tho I said nothing) as I had dictated the letter for the General's signature. Hermann is a charming chap, one of the oldest Italian families, a Marchese, tho' that's nothing against him—and a ripping good pilot. This last is a very important qualification and as an observer I can speak with feeling for I've been up with all kinds—good, bad, and indifferent. Sweetheart, you can not imagine what a boon your wonderful gloves and the suede vest were for, believe me, it was many times more than cold. If there were drawings to be made, of course, I could use the gloves— . . . One of the things which always impressed me, however, was the noise—especially the Caproni with 3 engines. Sometimes came home quite deaf and no amount of cotton wadding seemed to do any good. But this was only temporary so don't worry—you'll ask me if I enjoyed flying—I'll make you a confession—that I was really quite crazy over it—though one's degree of enjoyment always depended on several factors—weather conditions, and—above all—the pilot. The machine, too—the engine—you couldn't make up your mind to be entirely comfortable unless the motor was turning over properly. I am now counting on leaving Paris Friday or Saturday if possible (at latest Tuesday, the 4th)—will go straight to Florence, to Rome on the 10th and to Genoa for the 12th & 13th. Hope the boat comes in on time. Then to Rome for the concerts. Possible one concert in Milan early April and one in Florence about middle of April. This will be a large sufficiency.

Wednesday, 26 February 1919
Hotel Continental to 375 Park Ave.

Just a line to tell you that passport is obtained pour l'Italie en route for the U.S. and the visas too! My word! But you do have to stand in a procession – first, the Embassy, the French Prefecture, then Italian Consulate. After all the formalities one feels more like a criminal than anything else. Called on Caressa yesterday (the violin dealer) – He was, of course, very interested to know what I was doing. I mentioned the Rome concerts and "Quel violon avez vous" he asks. I admitted that the only one I had was the little Hill (modern) trench violin, so the dear man opens up his "caisse" and says "Choisissez!" I was really embarrassed but ended up by accepting the loan of a beautiful Montagnana – a perfect specimen and fine tone – for a couple of months. As Father has to come up to Paris & London on business, he will bring it back to Caressa with him. So I am now finely munitioned and after a few days steady practice which I have been putting in my fingers are in surprisingly good condition.

Am dining this evening with Whitney Warren [architect, lecturer, and writer; friend of D'Annunzio] and Lt. Hermann at Cecile Sorel's. The lady carries her fifty summers lightly and is still charming and is an ardent pro-Franco-Italian which feeling I think we should stimulate as much as possible. The Jugo-Slavs have nearly hung themselves and I think that far-sighted people here are realizing the real and lasting value of preserving the best relations with Italy – their natural ally racially and geographically. The news about Clemenceau always better.

Have my berth engaged for Pisa-Florence on Tuesday the 4th. One day before then Hermann and I are going out to the Chateau Thierry-Rheims-Soissons sector. It would greatly interest me to see this and though I don't believe too much in the joy-riding over the devastated battlefields at the present time I shall be very glad to go. Fondest & dearest love to you always – I do want a letter very badly, and am wondering if the next postman is going to be kind?

Friday, 28 February 1919
from Paris

Chère Bien Aimée—Three letters yesterday—F., G., & H., dates Feb. 9th, 11th, & 14th. Needless to tell you how happy they made me—so filled with love and tenderness—and never fear for a moment, dearest, that I would not understand perfectly your point of view nor must you ever have the slightest hesitation or fear that our love is a pale discolored thing that can suffer from frankness—and also I am perfectly in sympathy with your attitude that now the war is over, and I am released, it is my place to come to you, not yours to come to me, especially as it would be an injustice to your dear mother after her generous self-abnegation re your going over before the Armistice. Was deeply touched by your sentiment in regard to welcoming me home as a soldier—and not as a civilian. Please God, dearest, I shall always be your soldier, and if I do not wear your colors on my arm, they are tied to my heart. Now as to another question which you put squarely up viz: our future life free from entanglement your views are my views absolutely in this matter and our life is our own. The case is *absolute* not *relative*—no discussion necessary on this point. This I say in full recognition of family ties and interests. I would be lacking in frankness and sincerity by not admitting the close love and devotion which has always held us (Spaldings) together as a family and which I could no more forswear than I could my Americanism. I say this to you with a sense of pride—and with no fear of being misunderstood. It can no more be a point in question than your rather analogous position could ever be a point with me. Nor is it irreconcilable with my statement a few lines back. Our lives are our own not *relatively*—but *absolutely*—that you could have the doubt that I can not and do not decide for myself is only due to the fact that separation and distance sometimes carry worse poison than calumny. Don't you feel this to be so? No, Mary dearest—our lives are our own. I am an independent man—you, an independent woman, and we have both waited for this very moment and it is ours for the taking.

You will marry me, not my family—and I YOU, *not your family*—However, I love your mother and Scott, find their company interesting and charming and hope our relationship will develop and *it must*, for the profit and pleasure it brings my mind and heart. It is the sum, and utmost of my aspirations to see a reciprocal development on the other side. Is this clear? Ever since knowing you, my dearest, you have been an influence in my life, sometimes perhaps subconsciously. But (shall I be frank?) this influence does not take the place of others — nor eliminate them, but comes as an enrichment, and all the greater enrichment because of its supreme importance in my life. I do not love music less — but rather more because of you — I do not love my family less, but cherish them more because of you. You must feel that — recognise this, it's part and parcel of your own beautiful nature. As far as I can remember the only thoughts and influences which you have *replaced* — eliminated — are evil ones. The others you have added to — and God bless you for it.

The dinner at Sorels the other evening with Whitney Warren & several "members de l'Institut" was most interesting. We dined off purple damask and weird lights made us look fit for the Grand Guignol, but interesting and profitable conversation on Art — and especially Italo-Jugo-Slav politics. The question of Italy in the Adriatic and the revindication of her just aspirations there should be in no way in conflict with the inevitable and well merited development of the Serbs — and the other Jugo Slavs, too — provided they can *and will* go of accord together. But more of this in my next.

Sunday, 2 March 1919
from Paris

In my last letter I said I would try and sum up what seems to me the real issues in the Italo-Jugo-Slav question — Jugo-Slav is a word or name lately come into being — it means Slavs of the South and should by rights include all the Slavic nations in the Balkan States — Serbs, Croats, Slovenes, Bulgarians, Bosnians, Herzogovinians, Montenegrins, Slovaks. The Jugo-Slav State (soi disant) was formed by a combine of Serbs, Bosnians, Herzogovinians (who are Serbs racially), Montenegrins, Croats and Slovenes. As far as the Serbs and Montenegrins are concerned, I am entirely in sympathy with them. They have fought valiantly in this war, been good allies and are entitled to every consideration and they will receive it. But when we come to the Croats and the Slovenes my sympathies work slower. I can not forget that they have fought, and many of them willingly, as some of the best soldiers and officers during 4 years against the Italians. And yet we find them today as the most pretentious howlers and loudest dissentors amongst the peace delegates of today. Let us consider for a moment their claims vis-à-vis the Italian claims and study them for a moment – take a map of the Adriatic and you will see clearly what I mean.

1st. Italy claims Trentino Trieste, Ventia Julia, which includes Istria, Fiume, and such parts of the Dalmatian Coast as are settled by Italian (old Roman & Venetian towns) – Zara, Spoleto – she fully recognizes Serbis, and, if you wish Jugo Slavia's need for an outlet to the sea, and the utmost of her aspirations does not deny this window. Many strips of the Dalmatian Coast are not included in Italy's demands, nor is the port of Ragusa – which is proposed as the Jugo-Slav seaport. Italy lays claim to most of the islands outlying the Dalmatian coast – from strategic reasons – and principally because the coast of Italy on western side of Adriatic is absolutely flat and defenseless, as Italy found to her sorrow during the present war.

2nd. Jugo Slav claims – all of Dalmatia, Istria, Fiume, & even Trieste & Gorizia – Let us take some figures:

Trieste – Population:	
Italians (racially)	118,959
Italian citizens of the kingdom	29,439
Germans, Austrians	11,856
Slovenes	59,916
Serbo-Croates	2,403
Fiume – Population	
Italians (racially)	26,000
Italian citizens	6,000
Magyars	6,400
Slavs	12,000

I haven't the figures of the other Italian towns in Dalmatia but . . .

Istria Peninsula – Population	
Italians	358,000
Divers	10,000
Serbo-Croates	171,000
Slovenes	267,000

Now let us not be confused as to the term Jugo-Slav. *They are not* a homogenous race – Croats, Serbs, Slovenes – they have always fought amongst each other – therefore any argument that, collectively, they have in Dalmatia a numerical superiority and for that reason will rule collectively is no guarantee in the face of centuries of history. Furthermore, let us not forget that especially of late it has been Austria's policy (and the Slavs willing tools to that policy) to urge Slav immigration to a large extent in Italian speaking territories. Thus we have it that since 1901 the Slav population of Trieste has increased, by a fictitious and perfidious political ruse, 37,000. But this does not alter the fact that the culture, the monuments, the progress, and the civilization of these towns and of Dalmatia is Italian – and has been Italian for centuries – just as Alsace-Lorraine is French, tho' I have no doubt that German (Prussian) policy has greatly increased the German population there, and a census taken from numerical point of view might bring doubtful results. Italy's cause in the Adriatic is *just* – and her control of that sea is a guarantee to our future – to the future at least of Western Europe. Italy desires to live in peace and in friendly commerce with her neighbors, but she will not brook support of claims, unjust claims, of a people (the Croats) who have been for years Austria's worst weapon against her.

Tues., 4 March, '19
On departure from Paris to Florence

Dearest – Just a scratch to tell you I am off for Florence – Arrive there (due there!) – Thursday, the 6th – Then to Rome for rehearsals and concerts. Will write you a real letter as soon as I arrive in Florence. This simply to send you toute ma tendresse et tout mon amour dans un doux baiser – no more mail from you, but hope for some soon in Florence. Do you know that d– – –d copyist never finished your songs – never mind – have started a clean copy myself which will finish and send from Florence. The Arthur Symons is the only one of the bunch really worth its salt – so I think – Je t'aime, je t'adore – write me often, Sweetheart, and make me happy till we meet – *Ton Albert*

Thursday, 6 March 1919
14 Lungarno Vespucci, Florence

Just arrived, and find your dear cable – what a trump you are – how absolutely unworthy I feel of such tenderness. All I know is that I need it and crave it. Had a fairly comfortable trip and no trouble at

Albert's 1735 Guarnerius del Jesu violin.

frontier about my wee trunk as I was and am still in uniform and shall keep it on for these short trips. Much easier and simpler to travel this way. Celeste and Ida – or "Celeste Aida" as I call them – greeted me blissfully. They have got the house in a presentable state for the "padrone" and the Signora. I must warn Father as I am sure Celeste is going to make a dive to kiss him at the station – and I'm sure Father prefers a softer cheek. I am enclosing a little snap-shot of me taken in my flying togs which may amuse you. But when I come home I have some bully pictures of Rome for you – taken quite low, and clear.

Carlotti telegraphs an important concert for the Società del Quartetto Milan – Sonate Beethoven, Lekeu (Belgian) and my Suite with Luba – Fee for me 1000 lire – doesn't sound much in American circles – but here it is regarded a very important fee and while I do not attach great importance to it, I think it rather a gratifying indication, and know you'll forgive my mentioning sordid details to you, my love. On Sunday, I go to Rome, and Tuesday to Genoa, then back to Rome Thursday—concert Sunday and another one at the Academy the following Friday. At this last I am playing a Sonate of Corelli, some unaccompanied Bach, my Suite and two short groups with Lulli, Couperin, Chabrier, Saint-Saens, and a Spanish Dance of Granados and a bit of Wieniawski to see if my staccato is in good shape. The violin dear old Caressa lent me is a jewel, though not to make me unfaithful to my Guarnerius. Shall I tell you a secret—or rather a confession? My honest opinion that my Guarnerius is the most perfect violin of its type in the world.

Monday, 10 March 1919
from Hotel Palace, Rome

Just arrived Rome—have been to the steamship company and they assure me a place for an early to middle of May sailing. Will cable you as soon as definite date is fixed. This is a great relief as I had feared more congestion over this route. Have seen Molinari already and he tells me a great expectancy awaits next Sunday's concert. I am glad to be playing the dear old Mendelssohn, perennially young, and a fresh breath of spring—and, dearest, really there is not a trace of stiffness left in my bow arm. No news yet from the oncoming parents—but the S. S. company has signalled the Canopic's passing Gibralter. So they will arrive Naples tomorrow and Genoa Thursday. I am going tomorrow night to Genoa and return here Friday morning. Accepted a dinner at the Embassy for Friday evening. The Pages [American Ambassador to Italy] have been more than kind and he very solicitous in expediting my passport for Italy. The passport reads for the United States, via Italy. Just now I am expecting visit from an accompanist for the Rome recital. The Milan and Ferrara concerts are sonata concerts with Luba—but Parma, again is alone. Would that the "Lady of my Dreams" were to be with me in these dream cities.

In Florence, was every evening to dine with the Traversos—She, dear Stella, is so enthusiastic over you—your beauty—your charm—etc., etc.—it makes me almost embarrassed—and happy at the same time. I feel myself so much ONE with you, dear Sweetheart, that I dare to usurp the pride which your unique qualities entitle you to.

The copying of your songs comes laboriously on. In the meantime I have polished off the "When June is come" and it's much better—tho' still not so good as the Arthur Symons. I have a hunch they will suit your voice, dear heart. How happy I am that you are at your work again. We will work at the things together n'est-ce pas, ma cherissime?

Yes! my dear, I *have* read the *Four Horsemen of the Apocalypse* – thought it, by far the best novel of the war. Whitney Warren knew Ibanez quite well – was with him on the French front. He said Ibanez was a "queer duck" – often in a blue funk but always wanting to see everything. Still, the last person one would suspect of writing such a masterpiece. He does grasp the Psychology which war has wrought in French families of that type. Does it seem possible that we are actually approaching le gran jour heureux? Hold me – ye Gods of Reason – my hand is shaking at the thought of it – and my heart – better not to speak of it – Je t'aime à la folie ma cherissime – *Toujours ton Albert qui t'adore*

Tuesday, 11 March 1919
Albergo Palazzo Roma

Carissima mia – Have just been again to S. S. Agency – they promise definitely passage on one of the White Star liners in early May, but dates are not fixed yet – But I do feel easier now – and shall feel easier yet – when the passage is actually booked and date set. Called on Cortese, too (Assoc. Press Rep. for Italy). He promises to cover the Sunday concert well for the Amer. papers. They are doing three American compositions – Parker, Stanley Smith, and Arthur Foote – all of them good men – though I should have preferred something by Carpenter and Loeffler. These last two strike a more personal note and express modern American intellectual thought admirably. Did you ever hear Carpenter's Suite "The Perambulator?" Quite unique in its way, I think.

If the trunks from the States fail to arrive in time, I shall have to play the first concert in uniform – or in a business suit. Have no dress clothes here until my people arrive. The violin Caressa lent me is going finely – really a beautiful instrument – and peculiarly suited for the Mendelssohn concerto – tone limpid and crystalline purity. It will be real fun to do the last movement – Molinari is a good conductor and so things should go swimmingly – I almost feel as though I were making a debut all over again. All of my love in a long tender kiss – J'ai tellement besoin de ton amour ma bien aimée – *Toujours ton Albert qui t'adore*

Thursday, 13 March 1919
Hotel Royal Aquila, Genoa

Such a trip and what a disappointment on arrival Genoa. *Canopic* due here yesterday or today will, instead, not arrive until Friday or Saturday. What a muddle—Now I have to return to Rome tonight for rehearsals. Enfin on doit toujours avoir de la patience, but it is a shame.

Had a rehearsal yesterday afternoon with my accompanist who is to play for me at the Accadèmia on the 21st. Excellent he is, and the things go quite well. Have programmed the Suite—also some Corelli, Bach, Chabrier & Saint-Saens. Imagine my dismay yesterday—I found that one of the pieces of virtuosity I had programmed—a study Caprice by Wieniawski—had no pianoforte accompaniment. Partly out of curiosity and partly from interest I took 3 hours and wrote one. Ça n'a pas trop mal réussi and it was really good fun doing it—no tour de force—and not the way to produce a work of art—but the accompaniment is really quite sprightly and not banal, I think. The only thing I grudged to it was the taking of 3 hours away from copying and polishing your songs. You'll think me a fraud all the way through.

No clothes for concert. I shall either have to play in uniform or hire a dress suit. Don't feel like using the uniform for professional purposes—even though I'm allowed to—provided one wears the discharge red chevrons. But my decision will depend on what kind of a dress suit I'll be able to hire. Mrs. Page . . . is all of a flutter over the idea of the American compositions and adopts towards them that apologetic attitude which we too often find in our society patronesses. I couldn't help telling her that the success or nonsuccess of this or that American composition should not alter the faith which American music *per se* has a right to expect from our representative people. "But surely" she asks me "You would not want me to trumpet praise of bad or mediocre music simply because it was American." And I—"No! only to refrain from a prejudicial condemnation or apology until it had, at least, been heard." Perhaps I would have had more patience with the lady if she hadn't just established the speed of her musicality by declaring that the most artistic thing she had heard that winter in Rome was a transcription of "Handel's 'Largo' played by violins and harps"—An accurate portrait with a few charcoal lines—what? And these are the people that usurp the position and power (commercially at least) of arbiters! And yet I have faith in the actual love of music of even the untrained public. It's the badly trained parasites we ought to discount. I don't say that an untrained mind grasps or even enjoys specialized types of music — like for example Debussy or Ravel — there is a texture — a surface quality that exacts an ear training — as the early Siennese painters or a Japanese print requires an eye training. But the Venus de Milo, or a Beethoven Symphony — a Bach Choral — speaks everybody's language. Everybody at least who haven't vitiated their natural appetite with false stimulants and faddish narcotics.

A real cigarette famine in Italy though I manage to secure some by hook or crook. You see a line — longer than the bread line these days — that means they are on sale. Of course, a deal of traffic and profiteering in this as in other commodities. Perhaps you don't think of cigarettes as a commodity and are as well pleased as not at the famine. To which, O my enchantress, I reply — that having no real portrait of you other than the tiny snaps (and of course the one on my heart) — there is an ecstatic vision of you in each cloud of smoke and it has the azure tint of Heaven.

Celeste asked me anxiously if "la bella Signorina" was not coming, too? I asked him for fun to be precise — and he said La Signorina Pillay!!!!! Quite disconsolate that he was not to see you — "Tanta bella e tanta Simpatica lèi" (and this perhaps for him the most important) "tanta elegante!" Not bad for Celeste, eh!

Saturday, 15 March 1919
from Rome

Dearest — Returned from Genoa yesterday morning and since then have been on the steady go. Have had time however to complete copying and polishing your two songs and they are going to you in this same mail. Let's hope the censor doesn't suspect some deeply coded message and as such purloins the poor innocent music.

Have had two rehearsals with the orchestra and two with my accompanist for the Friday recital. The Mendelssohn goes swimmingly and Molinari gives me a very sympathetic back-ground. In point of view perfection of form — it is undoubtedly the finest concerto written and there is a lyrical quality all the way through I never tire of. The American compositions which Molinari has chosen are, I think, unfortunate selections — but O! it has so much the oily smell of college professors in its conventionality. As for the four Foote pieces, they are

Return to the concert stage, March 1919.

unspeakable. I asked Molinari what on earth he was thinking of to pass up Loeffler, Carpenter – and even Hadley – for this stuff. He pleaded a lack of necessary instruments – indeed "La Mort de Tintagiles" by Loeffler needs a good viola d'amore and where does one find them nowadays. Question of clothes for tomorrow settled. Am wearing a very good looking dress suit loaned me by my tailor here – and lucky it should be such a good fit. Called on the Cortesis – left them their tickets. They will cover the concert by cable to the "Times" and to the Associated Press. In return I have promised them an interview on the situation – Italo-Jugo-Slav. When I shall have the time to make the necessary notes, I don't know – though I have now quite a number of useful statistics – a column will be sufficient, I presume – not good policy to overdo.

I suppose you saw the draft of the Italian claims which was presented to the Peace Commission. I must say I was greatly impressed by their moderate and just demands. Italy asks for nothing that can not be fully sustained from geographical, ethnological, historical, civilizing – even racial reasons though the program does include the incorporating of some alien – Slav & Teuton, & even Magyar population into the Realm. But whereas the program of Poland means the inclusion of 30% alien population – and the other allied countries' scaled-down Italy appears to have the most unpretentious demands of them all with only 3% alien population. Did you see D'Annunzio's last message? Of course, he does occasionally slop a bit into dramatics – but who has the right to talk if not he?

I shall send you a draft of my interview after preparing it. Probably it will not touch a popular sentiment in the States – but then what's the use of living if you always let yourself drift with the stream if it's against your conviction? Per sempre e sempre tuo – amor mio – *Ton Albert qui t'adore* –

Sunday, 16 March 1919
Albergo Palazzo Roma

Just a dash of the pen, dearest, before leaving. The concert was a whirlwind – far beyond expectations. Can safely say the Mendelssohn Concerto never went with me so well. No exaggeration to say a veritable triumph. There's a rule of "no encores" at these concerts, but it was a riot – and so I had to play four extras – two Bach pieces, a Granados dance—and a Fauré Berceuse. Now I'm off for Florence—not a word yet from my family—don't know if they be arrived or not. But the mails and the wires are hopeless. I thought of you while playing—you dear inspiring angel—and the last movement of the Mendelssohn, which is like a breath of spring, could be a Botticellean overture to our dream.

Tuesday, 18 March 1919
from 14 Lungarno Amerigo Vespucci, Florence

My darling—Well! They're here—after many "pasticci" and missing telegrams, etc. Main tout est bien qui finit bien! Your two dear letters of the 25th & 27th just received—Mother brought the one—and the other came remarkably quickly—But why! O why! do you call me a Turk? If I were a real Pasha would I be so insistent on marriage, eh what? (to use your own expression). Dearest Love, what a lot we've both of us spilt over something that our two pair of eyes and two hearts will decide in two minutes. About my sailing! Think I'll probably sail in the first fifteen days of May on the Canopic. Father and Mother do not want to go quite so soon and will probably return in June, but I can not and will not wait until then—Stella Traverso will probably sail with me and we have both of us bespoken our passage. I note that your mother has rented the Bernardsville house, and—and are you really terrified at the idea of getting acquainted? I'm not—you know I'm a most reasonable and accommodating person—and not really a Turk! *No my dear* my mind doesn't change. That is—it changes about many things—but never about you—you darling. It was a grand reunion—and absolutely unclouded by any discussions of any kind or description—and, dearest, never imagine or worry for a moment that I repeat anything you may say to me. Even if my own good sense did not forbid it, my regard for you would. My love for and trust in you is far above any of the pit-falls or intrigues that even friends or family affections can sometimes dig for lesser attachments—and that your feeling for me is the same as evidenced by your dear cable and letters is a promise of Heaven for us both—pas vrai?

Rome, the 20/3/19

Broke off in the midst and am continuing now. Since writing the above has come your splendid letter of March 4th – in which you voice so beautifully what I feel but can not say. Of course, I'm thinking of June. I've dreamed about it and sung about it – and now you flash a woman's perogative before me – you Vixen! Don't push me to the wall too much about being a Turk – or I'll up and *spank you*. They say that's a Turk's perogative!

Papers here in Rome are very fine – am trying to find some extra copies – Have only one set as yet to which I hold on till I have others. They roast the poor American comps. The EPOCA says tho': "A real & enthusiastic success was obtained in 2nd half program by the Amer. Viol. A.S. in the masterly performance of the Mendelssohn Concerto – Spalding has a tone of power & sweetness – impeccable technic, and finest interpretive qualities – was clamorously acclaimed having to play as extras Prelude & Gavotte of Bach, and pieces of Granados & Fauré – to which succeeded interminable applause." The PICCOLO (principal paper): "On the other hand one can easily say of Spalding that in the aggregate of his musical qualities he is one of the finest living violinists – marvellous sweetness of tone, absolute purity in the most difficult passages, etc., etc." They're all of them enthusiastic and will send you the originals tomorrow. You know, in spite of my hesitation to write you these bombastic details – I too realize, my darling, that it is not fair on my part after all the proof you have given me not to have written you – not to write you more than actual details – and you will know that I don't do so from any vainglorious feeling, but only because I realize how you must share in vital interest in all of them – So that which would be conceited for me to write to anyone else – and probably bore them – I can – and must – write to you – n'est-ce pas – ma cherissime? Je t'aime à la folie ma cherissime and send you a dear tender hug and kiss.

Friday, 21 March 1919
from Rome

My darling: Just back from rehearsals and really the little chap does very well with my Suite which is difficult for piano. The hardest thing was for him to get the ragtime rhythms of the Vivace through his head.

But now it actually goes and I feel fairly safe with him. Dined last evening with Hermann's family, the di Targiani, typical Italian interieur—patriarchal system, and cousins and aunts galore. The old grandmother wanted to know if I was married. Disappointed by my negative reply "fiancé peut-être!"—and more encouraged to know that it was so—"Americaine?" Yes—"Jolie et charmante?" Yes—"Elle comprend l'Italien?" Yes—So they heartily approved, even without knowing your name.

Am taking tomorrow morning's train—7:20—back to Florence, but shall only be there for a day before leaving for Ferrara and Milan. At Milano will stop with Mrs. Esterle. My concert there is a Sonate recital together with Luba. We do the Beethoven 5th—my Suite—and the Lekeu Sonate (modern Belgian).

O irony! You write me so much and so often about the "League of Nations" and I realize that I have scarcely said anything in reply. Of course, I am in sympathy with it. It is a beautiful abstract idea that may be possible to put into practical form. I hope so. Perhaps I would have more faith and more practical enthusiasm over it if our dear politicians and diplomats could show more of its spirit and ideals in dealing with the burning and urgent present questions. In other words—let's clear up the actual situation and start with a clean slate before discussing Utopia. The surest guarantee for it would be a speedy accord amongst the Allies and a prompt signing of the Peace.

Sunday, 23 March 1919
from Europe Palace Hotel, Ferrara

Rome recital was as fine as silk—and Suite well liked—fairly well in the papers—they take a dig at some of the rhythms—which to my mind are the chief interest or raison d'être. A sweet letter awaited me in Florence on my passage through there. I shan't quarrel with you, my love, for railing at the selfishness of men. It's quite true. We are a self-centered, egotistical, obtuse race. These are traits which in some men become qualities—in others vices—and yet—taken as a whole—they are not unlikeable—unliveable—and they can be impersonal to a degree, which is also a relief—don't you think? As to women—they are wonderful—you justly say WOMEN—not females! I am content to call them wonderful without seeking to analyse. At the risk of appearing indifferent, which I am not, I dare to admit that I do not understand them, but I love them! Like Anatole France's dog "Il faut les adorer sans chercher les comprendre – leur sagesse est mystérieuse!"

Arrived here at Ferrara last night – Luba came from Milan – is now at the theater rehearsing. I have escaped the inevitable committee and their proposed banquet, and I am writing you from the dingy little hotel writing room – feet frozen, but heart warm with love. Ferrara is the Italian 13th, 14th, & also 15th centuries at their best. The castle of the Estes climbs over the other roofs and designs a wonderful skyline with its imposing towers and battlements. There is a line from Tasso at every street corner – and one has no difficulty in understanding whence came the culture that Isabella took with her to Mantua and Beatrice to Milan. The cathedral is a sympathetic marriage of Gothic and Roman – insofar as façade is concerned, but Alas! the theatricalism of the Baroque interior! Failing Catholicism imposed this, as it did in so many other instances. We can imagine hearing Michelangelo cry out "Alas for Art!" when the simple but majestic plans of his original St. Peter's had to be modified to cater to a vulgar and sensual taste.

Tragedy! No cigarettes and I am down to my last one. Not even the worthless little Macedonias can be obtained. It's now months that we've had this "crise de cigarettes" in Italy. Do you sympathise, or are you wickedly pleased that I am forced to shut down on the smokes? Fair – and cruel! I can almost feel your satisfaction!!!!!

Father leaves Florence for London and Paris next Saturday. As I shall not be home, I left the Caressa violin with him to return. I now have my own Montagnana. It's a beautiful fiddle, but lacks the "punch" of the Guarnerius (safely locked up in N.Y.) – Felt it unwise and unsafe to have that one brought over. The Montagnana has a pleasant, lyrical tone, slightly nasal in quality, but which is sympathetic to me. The Caressa Montagnana was less open in tone – family liked it better, undoubtedly I could exchange – but do not like to – Martie [Martie was Albert's maternal grandmother] bought this violin for me years ago – on my debut in Paris, and I feel it to be almost like a mascot. My dear, I know you don't believe it, but I am absurdly sentimental even to a superstitious degree. Then go and spoil it all in the end by usually doing the practical thing. This produced probably two things. In the first place, I have no illusions left – or only very few – I don't mean ideals – I have those a plenty of them – You should know this – you are the aggregate of those ideals. In the second place, the "life beautiful" as I understand it, consists of a reconciliation of the Life Spiritual and the life material. I believe thoroughly in the possibility and even the necessity of living one's life "beautifully" and this can only be the result of an inner evolution of spirit, struggling *not against things* – that would be wasted energy – but struggling against yourself – or that part of you which is affected – embittered by things. That you feel and understand this is another evidence of that Heaven on Earth which you bring to me. No! my dear! I do not know the Maeterlinck play – not this one at least. Strangely enough, I've not read a line of Maeterlinck for an age or more – He is one of the great mystics – and in some ways the finest living writer. He is that which so many others try vainly to be. For pure mysticism the "Princess Maleine" has not a peer, I think. I once made some sketches for incidental music, but they never became more than sketches. One would need a diamond pointed pen and thought of transparent ether and I have neither the one nor the other – only good enough sense to know that I have not.

Tuesday, 25 March 1919
from 47 Via Boccaccio, Milan

Imagine – nine hours travelling from Ferrara to Milan – poky miserable train – Ferrara concert was charming – and most successful. Had an "adventure" – finding that my Sarasate piece had been lost (the Romanza Andaluza) and it was programmed – I was in quite a pickle for provincial people are always touchy over a change of program. Fortunately, my memory stood me in good stead so the night before (Sunday night) I copied the entire score from memory – très bien réussie – It took me till half past two in the morning to do it – and I took a nasty cold "drat it!" with the stone floors and no heating, but the cold is nearly gone now – and the situation saved.

Had a pleasant morning here with Carlotti. He always remembers and asks about you – la bella giovane signorina Americana. You'll never dream what I read yesterday in the train – Mark Twain's Huckleberry Finn! and loved it. Never read it before – tho' of course Tom Sawyer was always one of my pets. Isn't it a relief and refreshing sometimes to go back to this pure narrative stuff after so much problem truck – like a good sea breeze after the heavy air of the desert.

In sending the songs I have not included the little Fanny Hastings' poem as that was not, or is not yet, successful. Will bring it with me – In the "When June is come" there is an optional ending. Use whichever you like best. The high ending is, of course, more effective, but should be done only with a sustained mezzo-forte – no clarion-like Jommelli ending! Have but very few signs & indications. Only enough to give general anticipation of the time – no strong dynamics necessary. Find quite a strong anticipation of the concert here. Nice program and really serious public. Carlotti had many things on the carpet also, but I've put on the brakes. Your advice is correct – I do need the rest and will try and fatten up a bit for my homecoming.

Luba has had a great Milan success, justly deserved. She should have, I am convinced, a fine career – if only she keeps her health – and her head! It was such a relief to find all my civ. clothes (dress suit, cutaway, etc.) in such good condition. Quite an item saved not to have to do any replacing. You have spoken of the possibility of your mother's taking a house in Maine for this summer. It's charming up there, but don't you think that it's quite a ways from New York – however, this summer's plans shall hinge around your wishes, dearest, and I am agreeable to everything that leads to your happiness – even if you do find me Turkishly adamant about the postponement of the marriage! *Toujours ton Albert qui t'adore*

Thursday, 27 March 1919
from Milan

Dearest Mary: There is very little to write – as I have no letter of yours to answer – and I am sure that you will be sick of hearing me say that which never tires me. My love and constant thoughts are with you every moment waking or dreaming – You are convinced – aren't you, darling, of our approaching happiness. If I have my way (and I shall, for you'll believe it, too), you will be so surrounded by love and tenderness that there will not be room for another sentiment. And you are going to be such a great help to me in every way – You are already now and always will be – an inspiration, but in our life together you are going to be a real material help – Your tact, your beauty of soul & body, your accomplishments and ready sympathy. For my own part I have that protecting feeling that I would wish to hide from you all but the enjoyment, but on the other hand I know that you would never consent to that and will want to take an active share in all the responsibilities, n'est-ce pas? and you can't know what a support and a help it will be.

There are sometimes dull and boresome things to do and dull and boresome people to see, but as long as we are together, our life can never be dull or boresome, what? Besides, darling, I too have the desire to put the brakes on too much public playing and slavishness to it. After all, we have our lives to lead and we might as well enjoy while we are young and can – and I see no reason to sacrifice everything for extra gain or what not. In one way the Wolfsohn contract is a Heaven sent thing as it lifts many responsibilities and worries from me. Then, too, I do think that they are by far the most dignified and conservative agency now in our country – don't you? Scott wrote me of his conviction that you were so much wrapped up in my art and would be a real help and benefit – as if I had ever doubted it; on the other hand, dearest, you must never doubt my tender and devoted love of you – it is this mutual trust which is the only thing that really counts. As for my not having spoken to you about flying – I'll confess with sore contrition – that I was completely wrong. I should have told you, but was an arrant coward thinking to worry you needlessly – and then never sure it would continue. Of course, if I had been sent to the front as was the intention if the war had continued, I would have told you, and then when the armistice was signed and I coming home, I had thought to keep it a secret until I saw you. Another reason, too, was my desire to keep from any publicity work (George Brown's enthusiasm) [on my] army career episodes. Of course, I know this would have been as distasteful to you as to me, and never would have mentioned it – well, anyway – I should have told you – so ask all abject forgiveness – non lo farò mai piu!

Carlotti has asked me in regard to South America for the summer of 1920, but I am holding him off. Told him to write me to America a definite proposal, but I wanted to see you first – and if you would rather not consider it, there is always time to refuse or postpone to another year. Of course, I would not think of going unless you cared to come with me. And, besides, after a good long season of work we might both want a good jaunty holiday – qu'est-ce que tu dis?

Saturday, 29 March 1919
from Milan

Yesterday's concert was a veritable triumph! Packed house, extremely interesting and intellectual public – and tremendous enthusiasm. Am enclosing a couple of the notices which were all excellent. The COR-

RIERE is the most important Italian paper—has almost an international importance. Everything went finely and Luba played beautifully, but perhaps the greatest success went to Bach and Corelli. The Suite interested more than it pleased. Played two encores at end of program after much and insistent applause. Now I am in a quandary as the Quartetto want to re-engage me for an orchestral concert (me alone)—I made the terms on purpose high hoping they would refuse, but am afraid they will accept. In case I do this it would be together with Padova and Verona (do you remember dear Verona?) and I would play Handel, Bach and Mendelssohn. It would come about April 15th ma poi basta. Curiously enough I have never found people so anxious to have me play as now when I am really quite indifferent to it. But that pur troppo is the way with human nature. My violin behaved beautifully, absolutely no "wolfing" in spite of two years' inactivity and the Bach really went as you would wish it, I think. O! ma cherissime.

Mrs. Esterle has been very sweet and I have been made very comfortable and at home. She always asks after you with great empressement. She is very good to Luba—and Luba will succeed—if only she wasn't at times such a Russian volcano. I am very fond of her, but really I do feel at times as though a steam roller had passed over me. C'est marcher à la quatrième vitesse tout le temps. If only she doesn't lose her head and commit some folly, she should have a fine career—mais!!

Sunday, 30 March 1919
Grand Hôtel Savoia-Majestic, Genoa

We are guests here of Ing. Negri & his wife—Negri was a former suitor of Luba—but when she up and married Giulio, he consoled himself by making many millions—and marrying a very charming girl (Miss Pirelli, of Pirelli's tires). He was a partner of Senator Esterle—very intelligent chap. I sometimes wonder if Luba regrets having refused him. Sent you the Milan notices yesterday—very good ones. Do hope the music manuscripts go through all right. I didn't send them from Rome as first announced but from Milan last week. Some minor changes which you will note from the sloppy scratches, etc. Have just read some entertaining books—French sketches "While Paris Laughed" by Leonard Merrick—the Irvin Cobb "Glory of the Coming"—(this was excellent). And have you seen Ambassador Morgenthau's book? By far the best on the Turkish situation 1913-1916. A rather weak though mildly interesting novel by John Galsworthy – "The Country House" – probably an early work – and a few pages of the Spectator. Nothing like train travel to make you read. Instead when we travel together, I shall sit at your feet and you'll tell me wondrous tales, O my Sheherazade! A thousand and one nights and then begin all over again. Can you not imagine how charming it will be. We'll shut the world and everything else out – and alone in our own intérieur (for we can have a real intérieur even in a Pullman compartment!) we'll build our own palaces of dreams.

Am afraid the Milan concert is going to take place after all – I wonder if it's a weakness that makes me accept it – Enfin – as Sambo says "Dis 'am de final las!"

Monday, 31 March 1919
from Milan

Called this morning at White Star Line. Had a very satisfactory talk with the agent and he is quite sure there will be no difficulty about my place on the *Canopic*'s next sailing. Without guaranteeing, he assured me that they would take care of me one way or the other. Father has left for England. Will do his best to return by way of Italy if the powers that be give him necessary visa or passport. But they do make such a fuss about it. There are more "joy-riders" around than you can shake a stick at, but innumerable difficulties for people who have legitimate interests. Wretched travelling these next two days, leave here tonight midnight – arrive at Vicenza tomorrow 5 A.M. Tomorrow evening concert & leave Vicenza the following morning 5 A.M. for Padua – change there at 6:30 for Bologna – and another change there at 1 – arriving in Florence at 5:30 – Ma Pazienza – the travelling conditions are what they are and kicking about them won't do any good. But how easy it will seem to travel again in our own fine trains –

Had a pleasant day yesterday in Genoa with Ing. Negri & his wife (just married) – After the concert they drove us out to the villa Negri has bought. On a bluff overlooking the Mediterranean and with Geneva la Superba in the distance. It's a veritable dream place with terraces, & grottoes – and always the sea framed by your own favorite green of cypresses – Negri insists that we come to visit them – you and I – don't think he knows your name, so calls you "la bella sposa Americana" – on our next trip to Europe. Mrs. Negri – reserved, a bit shy, but très fine would, I think appeal to you. They had with them Mrs. Paolo Tosti (widow of the erstwhile popular composer of ballads) a charming old Belgian lady who rather startled me by asking out of whole cloth if I was in love – and explained, after my admission that it was so, that she knew it – and to my "Why?" answered "because you are far too distrait – no musician is really modest" (this was a sad blow!) "and here I've been talking steadily about you – and you've not heard a word I've said" – which was true.

Thursday, 3 April 1919
from 14, Lungarno Amerigo Vespucci

Your letter from Yama Farms was awaiting me – and what a dear one it is – You brought the beauty, the peace and quiet of the place to your pen – and it's through the interpretation of your own rare nature that I enjoy the fragrance of it all. Am just back from Vicenza – and look forward to a week's good quiet rest at home. Vicenza, delicious old town with its Ca d'Oro and market place recalling the beauty and the charm of Verona. But my O my! What a trip! Imagine, that from Milan to Vicenza, midnight to 5 A.M. I spent the entire trip in corridor resting as best as one could on the suit case. Glad to find a seat for Luba. Mais, on n'y fait à tout – one poor chap – an Italian officer got in struggling with his locker – "I'm fed up" he said, in excellent English. "Well!" said I "no use to frown – you might as well smile" and gave him a corner of the suit case. We had a pleasant conversation all the way – consumed innumerable cigarettes (he had a stock) & this was more than comfort – a necessity in view of the stench! At Vicenza, fortunately had rooms waiting and I slept solidly till midday – Fine concert and many officers and soldiers, some of them my old "fans" – violin students from the Scala days. A sweet little note from Marion Beckett from Paris which I have just answered – She must be a real girl if she's as good and straightforward as her writing. The Milan orchestral concert is arranged. Play there on the 12th – nice program. Porpora Sonate – old Italian, Chaconne of Bach – a group of character pieces – and the Mendelssohn Concerto to close with. The St. Cecilia Academy in Rome have asked for me again for the Kreutzer Sonate, Beethoven & Mozart, but I have refused. Time to say "Basta." Yes, dearest, the Wolfsohn contract is going to take a lot off my shoulders and make my time much freer – I shall be jealous of every moment not spent with you – & you will enter with such spirit into my work – n'est-ce pas – I love to think of you at Yama – and know what the rest will mean to you – Dearest darling, my heart goes out to you in a long and loving wave. I could almost be persuaded to believe in the occult (perish the word) so close do you seem to me – how beautiful your spirit makes this world of ours. *Love untold from your own Albert*

Sunday 6 April 1919
from Florence

My darling: Two delicious of the the 11 and 13 March, both from Yama Farms – One of them encloses a snapshot of you for which I am always, of course, hungry. This one looks as though you were auctioning off Liberty Bonds and has a worried troubled expression – the brow trying to frown and your sensitive mouth edging to a smile. Don't talk to me about the detail – it's good I suppose, but I am looking only at the face. These last two days I have been writing, writing feverishly. From the sketches made in Rome I have completely rewritten the 1st movement of the Sonata – some 300 bars or more – It is really good, I think, but then a certain discount must be made for composer's 1st enthusiasm. What makes creative work so fascinating is the illusion that one has invariably that "this" (the actual work in hand) is always the best effort. I have to write when the fever is on me, the only possible way to accomplish anything in big form. Well! I'll reserve my real opinion, until I can play it to you and have you to guide or to console me.

How I enjoyed your relating of the dream of being with me in our old house in 53rd St. How vivid they can be and then what a disappointment to wake up. Curiously enough while I was in Rome about that time (March 12th) I, too, had a vivid dream of you – and we were together in a house unfamiliar to me. It was much as you describe it – only instead of your "Mary" Welsh woman in the doorway, there stood Mr. Buitrago – he said "And so you are married, che cosa tremenda!" and we both laughed happily at his evident pleasure. We also had a long talk – and many things I can not recall – except a serene state of bliss, floating in ether – and nothing in the world seemed to matter but that you were you and I, I. Could we not almost call it "Dreaming True"? Now don't go and appall me with your suggestion of a time fuse and my arriving too late for the flame – You gave me visions of a vixenish Carmen singing:

Bel officier, Bel officier,
L'amour vous joue, en ce moment, un assez mauvais tour—
Vous arrivez fort mal! Vous arrivez fort mal!—

and it's all impossible and untrue—Then, too, remember that I am a Turk and shall carry you off by storm if necessary. So There!!!—Father is now in Paris—had a wretched time losing his trunk and in order to find it had to wait off in Modena, thus forfeiting his sleeper. Truly no joke, travelling nowadays. He will try and return to Florence early May—Am not sure if he and Mother expect to sail back with me—probably not, but will wait until June. Then, too, passage would be very difficult for them to obtain. Mine, praise be! is as secure as possible—and if not possible on the *Canopic,* I have a possibility of an Italian steamer. Your suggestion of the Caproni an excellent one if only the noise of 3 motors would not make me so deaf and I must be in position to hear your voice! On the whole I prefer the Arabian carpet. Am going on Wednesday evening in Milano—arrive there Thursday morning, fortunately have a sleeper, a boon nowadays—Rehearsals there with orchestra and accompanist—let's hope he's a good one. I do want to quietly finish the 2nd and 3rd movements of the Sonate. The adagio has a real Darky theme poignantly beautiful and simple and I am keeping the treatment of it rather archaic & simple—the finale is genuine ragtime—quite rollicky.

Tuesday, 8 April 1919
from Florence

The 1st movement of the Sonate has been entirely completed—and I think you will like [it]—Have also copied out Fanny Hastings' little song which I'll send to you from Milano. Have yet to put some conventional signs. This little song you must not take seriously. It's just a little musical joke—but bright and good for your voice—I think. Had meant to write you a long letter today, & should have done so, but I'll confess the real truth—I had a few more touches to put to the Sonate—and so wrote my words of love in the music. It's for you, my dear, that I worked—and am working—I love you tenderly, dearly—and, in another little month's time shall be speeding you-ward.

Thursday, 10 April 1919
from Milan

Dearest: Wrote you a little line last night from Florence just before starting. Had most comfortable trip in sleeper arriving this morning where Mme Esterle had me met by the automobile. Seems to be great expectancy and enthusiasm awaiting the concert on Saturday. House already sold out — and they had proposed changing to the large auditorium, but I counselled against this — as the orchestra is not large — only fifty pieces — Carlotti says he has had an urgent letter from the South American manager — desiring to fulfill the old contract. As I explained to Carlotti, while I did not wish to refuse this, yet to hold it in abeyance until we should decide together whether to accept it or not for the summer of 1920. Also to make clear that certain financial modifications must be made in the contract. 1st payment must be made in gold — as the Exchange is so fluctuating as to render this an essential. 2nd that I would want all travelling expenses paid — for 3 persons — 3rd that at least an anticipated guarantee of 15,000 lire (gold) be placed to my credit a month before starting. If he agrees to these three conditions we can always then decide if we want to do it in 1920, or 1921 — what do you say? I keep saying "what do you say" though your answer (praise be!) will be verbal and not in writing. I wrote to Rome refusing the concert for the St. Cecilia Society. They wanted the Beethoven Sonate "Kreutzer" & some Mozart. Also another manager has been besieging me for a tour in Venetia and on the Dalmatian coast. Very good terms, but this, too, I shall refuse. The Genoa concert I have agreed to take, only providing they make it coincide with my sailing date about May 10th or 12th. I am glad you liked the little *Times* notice of the Augusteo concert. Thanks, awfully, for enclosing it — I am sending you by this same mail the little song by Fanny Hastings. As I wrote you before, don't take it seriously. It's just a little "frou-frou" — you can be very free with the time — the piano interludes should go quicky — and less so the song. I am really pleased with the result of the Sonate. 1st movement, that is — I have the slow movement and Finale already sketched but not really satisfactory. Tonight is Luba's orchestral concert. She will, I'm sure, have a great success and due not only to her fine talent, but also to Mme Esterle's tactful and powerful protection.

There is an exceeding feeling of unrest — the latest developments of Bolshevism in Bavaria are more than disturbing — altho my feeling is that this is only a German ruse to evade paying all indemnity. And each hour of delayed decision on part of the Peace Conference aggravates this tension – The Pit of it all is that the leaders that be have completely lost the confidence of the people. But O my dear! I am so sick of politics – greed, dishonesty, unscrupulous ambitions masked by flowery phrases. The politicians seem to be bent on nullifying the sacrifices of four years and more.

Friday, 11 April 1919
from Milan

Dearest: Had two rehearsals, one this morning with the accompanist and the other at 1:30 with orchestra. Very satisfactory and I believe that the Mendelssohn should go as well as in Rome. Am almost persuaded to use this concerto as a re-entrance piece in New York. Damrosch has my first appearance (don't know the date yet!) and I have the feeling that the Mendelssohn will make a fine impression. Both the Beethoven and the Brahms have, it seems to me, been played to death and anyway my last performance with Damrosch was with the Beethoven.

Luba was in good form last night and made a great success with her two concertos – Beethoven E flat and Grieg. Her qualities are put in the best possible relief with orchestra, and certain drawbacks, as for instance, a too great insistence sometimes on obvious details, were not at all apparent. I have rarely found the Russian temperament so adapted for chamber music, and Luba is very Russian. The spring birds are all out – also here – serenading us and I am pretending as you suggested, that they are whispering words of love from you. Dearest, Sweetheart, you are such a child of nature that even a green tree seems to breathe of your presence. We must always have our fullest fill of the country – It's a tonic – the best kind!

There is a deal of Bolshevist agitation, but so far under good control. Was glad to see that in Rome the sensible element got together and on the very day of an anarchistic demonstration the reactionists made a counter demonstration and, as fortunately they were in the majority, had all the advantage. In fact, the Bolshevists were very considerably worsted and many of them got severe beatings for their pains! – Bravo for Rome! I say, that if there's any real fighting and shooting to be done — let's us be in on the first. I know that we are in the majority (the people who desire to preserve peace & order) and therefore we are the real representatives of democracy. Of course, all this agitation & unrest is constantly fed by the indecision and delays of the Peace Conference. It is with no desire nor intention to criticise the powers that be, for I fully realize the gigantic task which they have to contend with, but it is after all reasonable to feel impatient at the introduction of so many irrelevant and misleading matters before the real problems are first solved. The League of Nations can not be practically brought into effect unless the nations who have been bound together by mutual aspirations, interests, & sacrifices can decide to agree amongst themselves. I am getting to that point where I feel like saying, "Any decision, O Lord! but let's have a decision!" In the meantime, until a decision is reached and some return effected towards normal conditions, business enterprise is quite paralysed. Money which should be in circulation goes into the stocking — stagnant — because until the fog of uncertainty is lifted, and people can see clearly what can — and what can not be done, no one will risk money. And with the necessity of increased & continued taxation in our country — and especially in Europe — it should be the most urgent concern of the Government to see to it that everything be done to maintain and stimulate all legitimate business enterprise so that the taxes imposed will find the necessary response. Did you see James M. Beck's latest declarations re. the League of Nations? He does hit the nail so perfectly on the head. But here let me put on the brakes, for me thinks I see my love yawning with ennui at my political harangues!

Saturday, 12 April 1919
from Milan

I am imagining to myself that your love and tenderness is surrounding me — and so — am happy. Milano is shining its prettiest — as a rule foggy & rainy (they call it the Italian London), we have, instead, had beautiful sunny days. This morning — last rehearsal with d'Erasmo — Finding yesterday that no proper edition could be had of the Schumann "Abendlied" which I have programmed this evening, I made myself a special arrangement last evening — simple and in the original D flat instead of the D natural which most of the violin transcriptions carry.

The D flat is so much softer and makes quite another picture — anyway it was only the work of two hours, but d'Erasmo, when I put the manuscript (in my best calligraph) before him seemed overwhelmed: "What," he exclaimed, "on the eve of a concert you had the energy and nerve capacity to do this work." I explained to him that it was in reality no work, but, dearest, I am convinced that he found it remarkable only because in general solo artists are so lazy — and such slaves to their nerves — Ugh! I hate the class. Life is too short — and too many real things to be enjoyed! Also there are a tremendous lot of fine performers — technically and tonally, I could name quite a list of both fiddlers and pianists who play quite perfectly — but unless they are interesting people, themselves, and have something really personal to say — and in a natural, simple manner what does it all amount to? I wrote you some time ago, during the war, of feeling strangely detached from my music — or no! not from music but rather from that intense concert life which once seemed so absorbing. Well! I find that this detached feeling continues — the pleasure in playing is as keen as ever, perhaps more so, but I am convinced that the old absorption, almost obsession for public playing — and public success — will never return and I'm glad of it. It would be a pose for me to say that I am indifferent to applause or public appreciation once I am playing. Part of your nervous force in a performance is derived from this, but the point is, my Mary, to rid your mind of the fact that the "public" as such has any real musical opinion of worth. Individuals sometimes have, but the public collectively, never! Don't you find that even excellent artists are so often ruined by this slavish devotion to "what the public thinks" or "what the public wants"? Genuine criticism does not exist. And as a rule most of the reports one reads of musical performances are as half-baked as are the performances themselves. The real taste for music in our country must be developed by the intelligent lay-men, and I am happy to believe that this class is really increasing with us. But this is produced and developed *only by* individual effort. The much trumpeted community chorus will not help it. This is only an abortive attempt towards a sort of glorified mediocrity. It appeals to the Ego in inviting active participation. But active participation by the masses, means a disastrous musical result and furthermore (which is worse) kills the faculty for developing an intelligent perception. There is and can be no such thing as "Democratizing Art" that much abused phrase. Art is the aristocrat and individual expression of a soul in search of beauty. It is within the reach of all (rich and poor) and in that sense is Democratic — Well, the sun, moon, and stars are democratic in the same sense. But our reaction to these things are, if of value, an individual, not a collective reaction.

Tuesday, 15 April 1919
from Verona

Dearly Beloved: I'd like to write you only in verse and in couplets from — shall we call it the Cradle of Modern Love? And that what I wish to do always outruns what I can do, so though it is not permitted to be " a glove upon that hand, that I might touch that cheek" — yet it's a blessed consolation that I *do* touch this paper, with my hand, that will touch yours.

The Milan concert was nothing short of a triumph. In good form, packed house and I had quite a glow from the way things went. The Chaconne especially seemed to grip the audience. I don't remember ever having been able before to so completely hold the concentrated line — there were always some ragged, broken sections. Three extra numbers had to be added long after the lights were out & I had thought to bow my last. Milan audience really a fine one. The next day was delicious — Mme Esterle took us to Como Lake — Villa d'Este & Cadenabbia. She kindly let me sit front seat with chauffeur which was a boon, not having to talk with anyone — and altogether a day of relaxation. I have read and greatly enjoyed the "Secret City" — A powerful vivid picture, sinister in spots but really a fine idealism through it all. How splendid the portrait — I liked it far more than the "Dark Forest" tho' this, too, was good. How real books can be — and what a part they can play in one's life — Often I find myself remembering places not so much by dates of sojourn, but by books read there.

Was half tempted to accept a couple of concerts in Trieste. They offered 2000 lire for the two concerts & I accepted providing they make them come together and give me 50% gross receipts as well — and furnish a good accompanist. Would enjoy seeing Trieste & ascertaining with my own eyes the true situation there.

The concert in Padova last night was good fun — many officers among others Lt. General Petitti — who was inspector general of Aviation and who was astonished to find in me the same Aviator-osservatore who had been so often to his office to bother him. He insisted on kissing me — both cheeks, a most painful operation to keep from roaring. This occurs so often — and the Italians love it as a public exhibition.

Whitney Warren has come back from Dalmatia more pro-Italian than ever — and is doing great work with his propaganda stuff in Paris. He is an enthusiastic worker if ever there was one.

Wednesday, 16 April 1919

En route for Florence — stopping off at Bologna. Ugh! What a trip — up this morning at 3:45 and down to the dingy station — Verona presented no very romantic picture at such an hour — And O my dear! You've no idea how dirty a station can be when over-crowded with troops on their way to or from leave — The canteens were busy dealing out soup, etc., but so messy — more of it went on the pavement than to its proper destination. Stray conversations one hears indicates more than anything else the impatient temper of the people with the delay and the uncertainty of the situation. Many of the criticisms are, of course, unjust but on the whole my impression is that they have been very patient. The next three or four months are to be the crucial time without a doubt — If these are tided over then we can hope for the return of something like normal conditions — But the government is certainly playing a risky game trying to sit on both sides of the fence at once.

Verona was disappointing as to audience. Not in size for the theater was quite full, but in attitude — Beethoven and Bach seemed to leave them quite cold and they only apparently waked up to some fireworks at the end — that sort of thing is like a wet blanket after the situation of Milan and Padova. Of course, a theater is never as adapted to the quieter sort of music as a hall.

Friday, 18 April 1919
from Florence

You ask what made me suggest and continually speak of June? So I'll "fess" up — In the first place I've been for a year or more continually dreaming of June, your June and mine — 2nd — in June 1918 I received from you a letter which perhaps for the first time disclosed the full depth of your love and your tenderness — not that I ever doubted it, but still I was greatly affected by the psychology of it. 3rd — your poems which you sent to be set to music sang insistently of June and this, too, stuck in my crop — 4th — June was the month your father & mother were married, wasn't it? Also, mine — ma cara — of course, I was a brute not to ask your preference first and foremost, so shan't quarrel at your scolding good and hard if you want to. I have stated all the reasons — sentimental ones which prompted June — but aside from this, it seems to me also to have a practical side, too — in that it gives us the summer, free and to ourselves. So now! I give you fair warning that I am going to be a very ardent persuader, perhaps you'll think me an unscrupulous one to take so much for granted.

Further on you say "It is awful, isn't it? — but I don't want to get married. But then I told you that here 18 months ago." etc., etc. No, carissima — who said that we were going to get married, and be married as such? Out upon it! We're going to be lovers all our lives — and on to the world beyond. The legal knot is a passing formality — same as we wear a dress suit to an evening party — but the real you — and the real I are *one* together already. Of course, I am "a real male being" and love to be loved and petted, but part and parcel of it is the opportunity of loving and petting some one dearer to me than myself. "Honest Injun" I'm not the selfish, brutish egoist you sometimes tease yourself into believing, but a most amenable, accommodating, and livable sort of a person. Full of faults which the influence of a loved one can do much to temper and a world of dreams for a loved one to stimulate.

What a gay time you had with your Elsie Fergusons, etc. [In regard to] the 2 married couples, as you say, "one a strangely selfish wife, and the other a very selfish husband" O you are perfectly right in your remark that the great stumbling block is if a man takes himself too seriously, or his work, or his art — that it is de-humanising. I know too that often, a man's absorption in his business or profession becomes an obsession out-focussing a true perspective on life and its real values — that this is [true] in 50%, perhaps more, of cases of matrimonial shipwreck is no secret — and the woman in giving her all towards the mutual happiness feels (not unreasonably) jealous of a rival, all the more exasperating because it's an intangible one. But this can not & does not happen if there is a fair amount of give and take on both sides — and especially (as you say) — a sense of humor to help it out. On the other hand, what the woman fails generally to recognize is that she makes a rival of what she loves best in the man — and in her jealous tyranny would destroy the very fountainhead of her own love. My darling, I have not spoken of our coming happiness to any but very intimate and dear friends, and be assured that I shall, of course, be very discreet, but don't be too displeased if I have spoken to these few. It seemed only right and natural and I never dreamed that it was contrary to your wish. I have found your emerald — and it's a pretty one — not very large but excellent color and very few feathers (they say that no real emeralds are absolutely free of them). Have it in a pendant of a pretty setting — rather simple, Louis XVI — and anyway it's your color, dear heart, and hope you will like it. My paper is out, and so also the light, nearly — but my heart is aflame with love for you and my fond goodnight is travelling down the [river] on the moon path — *Ton Albert qui t'adore*

Sunday, Easter Day — 20 April 1919
from Florence

There is no passage available on any of the Italian boats at present sailing and up to May 10th or 12th which is the time due for the *Canopic* sailing. Up until now the White Star Line report everything O. K. — for the *Canopic* sailing around May 12th and this is the best bet. Then I have a part option on a couple of the Italian boats (South American liners) which are to be put on U. S. service latter part of May. This is the eventuality of the *Canopic* falling down on me at last moment — or delayed sailing.

Had a sweet little letter from LaGuardia who went into extasies over you. He is now on the ocean coming over on some investigation committee or other. I suspect it is something on the line of what I previously wrote you — and am heartily glad to be in civ. clothes — no inclination to be drawn into such an affair.

Have been working hard on the Sonate — 2nd movement about whipped into shape. It's good, I think, but not the musical value of the 1st as to form. But the theme is a real plantation melody (never before transcribed) and is of poignant beauty — there is a sub-theme, also a negro song, which gives it a real American flavor. Who do you think I had a letter from yesterday? Coenraad Bos! Think he wrote from Berlin tho' the letter was posted from Holland. He expects to come to the States next autumn — and was feeling out the ground some — of course, I wrote assuring him "that *Dutch artists* would always be welcome especially when they were discreet and tactful, as I was sure he was!" He wrote that Mme Culp was getting a divorce from her

Mary and Albert . . .

. . . the betrothed.

husband and would marry a millionaire Austrian – sing only for charity henceforth. Perhaps she may change her mind about the millions – as the kronen is not worth a tinker's damn just now. I do hope the songs got through to you o. k. and that you could read my crabstick. I tried to be extra careful with the calligraphy for my Love.

Had Celeste get out my old tennis racket, and hope to have a few sets this week and get some good fresh air and exercise – the spring has been late in coming this year, but is now here with a vengeance. But I am almost jealous of any time spent away from my music – or writing to you –

Tuesday, 22 April 1919
from Florence

Wicked, wicked Vixen! Devilish Fairy Queen! I half suspect you're teasing me to death, dearest – and the next moment feel like taxing you with the gentle & subtle art of Fishing. but I'll be generous and only retort that you are talking thro' your hat when you say that "I don't need you one little iota" and that you'll be an added care and responsibility. This last, of course, you will be! I should hope so at least. I hardly expect to marry a disembodied spirit – ethereal as you are, my Love, and part and parcel of my happiness is the responsibility and care that could come from you. If you should ever have a care or a worry and dare to not let me share & shoulder it – I should be truly jealous – yes, really and stupidly jealous – and rage and stamp about – bite the bedpost and break the china – so there! But yours, darling, is the power of infinite love, infinite tenderness, and infinite spirituality, and the blessedness of this inspires me to know that I, too, have much to give you in the way of happiness, because I do understand you – and cherish you in my love.

Am still busy at work on the Sonate though it's not going so easily – so yesterday I took a holiday and wrote a frivolous little piece, touch of Iberia for my album of water colors. It's a fiddle piece, Spanish in character – I call it "Yankee Doodle in Spain." It may prove to be an encore piece as it has some rollicking rhythms.

Today was the first of our series of funerals – poor Mme Braggiotti and with slow means of locomotion – and considerable distances it occupied the best part of the day – Tomorrow or next day is Comm. Matteini's funeral. He, poor old man, was well over ninety and his passing came as a great release. I have no feeling of horror or even great grief at the thought of death—especially when it comes normally and at the natural close of life, but I do hate funerals they seem to me to be a medium for the worst display of hypocrisy that humanity is capable of. One sees the very people who most criticized and quarrelled making a show of feeling that they were far from giving to the same body when the spirit and soul was still there. Perhaps it's remorse, but I suspect it more of being arrant hypocrisy. My own creed is that the finest respect you can pay to the dead is to show a little more consideration and unselfishness to the living. There was an English Clergyman too who officiated and his sing-song voice and mannerisms robbed the words of the ritual of all their majesty, making a musical-hall pot-pourri out of a masterpiece of spiritual art.

Have had several more letters from Whitney Warren. He is back now in Paris and still busy on his work. Things are slowly straightening themselves out. Lloyd George's frank, open, and clear statement in the House of Commons purified the air—and if the politicians and the diplomats will now only think a little more of the good of their countries—& of humility, and a little less of future votes—all may yet be well! But as you say the unsettled condition of Europe is most alarming—and in view of this impending menace all local questions—including the Dalmatian coast, loses much of its former significance. My impression is that the next five or six months will decide the fate of rationalism, or Bolshevism (some wag called it "Bochevism" as it was the Germans who gave it birth and nourished it!) But even if Bolshevism does not prevail, great changes must take place. All intelligent people see this. The world can never again return to the same old inconsequential basis as before. We are our brother's keepers—whether we will or not—and it is realization of this or—cataclysm!—and a worse cataclysm than the war. Society will no longer be able to thrive merely by setting up arbitrary standards of right and wrong for the benefit of the favored classes of the Status Quo and taking relative measures for the alleviation of suffering and the punishment of crime. They must go further than this and strike at the causes of these two sister evils—and if it's not the responsibility of the favored classes—whose is it?

Thursday, 24 April 1919
from Florence

I am so pleased that you've taken up some Loeffler songs. He is the greatest tone poet we have in America. Don't know his songs, but am a profound admirer of his orchestral pieces and chamber music. Think it no exaggeration to say he is at present our finest composer. Did you ever hear "La Mort di Tintagiles"—?

Too bad, what you write of the Salzedo ménage, tho' I confess to not feeling greatly surprised. I do feel intensely sorry for Lola for it seemed to me that she loved him so devotedly and unselfishly. S. is a fine musician, but too arrantly an egotist and self-centered. This he has manifestly shown on many occasions—but I had hoped that a sense of appreciation for all that Lola has done for him would prompt a greater consideration and tenderness. Lola has never been "simpatica" to me and I do not altogether trust her sincerity of character (this of course strictly confidential), but I do admire the way she has conducted herself with her husband—ma basta—I do wonder if the songs ever reached you, fortunately I still have pencilled copies—and will make you a fresh pen copy—The "Yankee Doodle in Spain" had its last bar written just before starting this letter. It developed to be rather more than the bagatelle it started out to be.

Was down again to White Star agent who still could give me no definite news of *Canopic*, but said that the 15th was still fixed as ultimate date for its sailing—He gave me reasonable assurance that my booking would hold good as they have yet no indication that passengers will be excluded—and my name is the first on the list. However, not content with this, I went to the Italian line again, and definitely fixed a passage for the *Pesaro*—sailing toward the end of May, which I am permitted to cancel as soon as *Canopic* sailing is definite. The *Dante* has been booked solid for some time past. However, I now feel more relieved to feel absolutely sure of my passage tho' I should be distressed, of course, to have the *Canopic* fail and delay my starting another ten days or a fortnight. But it's good to be sure and I've drawn a real long breath—I don't like to say how really worried I've been—I had all along the conviction that anyway, by "hook or crook" I'd manage passage, but I've had several disquieting moments. And now that I am sure of the Italian passage, in all probability the *Canopic* will be O. K.—like taking an umbrella with you to scare away the rain. Boardman writes. . . that an interview with the Wolfsohn people shows a very satisfactory result. It seems they have practically already covered the 50 concert bookings which is the total amount guaranteed and are anxious to increase to as many more as I'll play. I am very pleased at the demand, but prefer to go slow. One season I did play as many as 108 concerts, but it was too much. Think not more than 70 or 75 – that makes an average of 10 or 12 a month for 6 or 7 months.

Was out today to Comm. Matteini's funeral. Poor Mary M. all broken up. She is now staying with us. Was devotedly attached to the old man, tho' he years older than she. But sometimes strange assortments make for a contented ménage. Shall now start in again seriously on completing the Sonate. The Spanish Caprice was a little holiday interlude and I am going back again to the bigger form, mentally refreshed. Of course, I am sane enough to realize that the Sonate is not successful from the highest point of view – but at least can feel that it's a sincere attempt at something big – and – as such worthy to inspire me to do better next time. Have been haunted lately by some themes, well adapted, I think, for treatment as a string quartette. It's been an encouragement to realize that more and more my thoughts are coming easier in the larger forms. I am still and shall always remain (I think) an "absolutist" in music. Modern idioms charm and enchant me but only in sequence of form and line. And more and more strongly, too, I feel this.

How splendid – all that you write of your voice and its development. Am looking forward keenly to playing your accompaniments. Have developed piano playing quite a bit so that with a bit of practise can manage most songs decently. Shall make you sing by the hour. You must sing often to overcome all feeling of nervousness and gêne. It's fine that Griffith has been able to liberate your voice and give it a freer attack. Don't think too much of the mechanism tho, except when you are practising. I have often found it a valuable help to use autosuggestion. In other words, while playing invoke some lovely image – not necessarily a musical one, and the tone floats out surprisingly free. It's only a means of liberating the mechanical production from a certain tightness that accompanies too much concentration and preoccupation on it. Of course, to do this you must have a considerable freedom from the mastery of the mechanics – but this you'll have. A thousand tender kisses, O my sweetest Mary, and a blessed love which grows with every hour of recognition of all that you are – dear – dearest – *Your own Albert.*

Saturday, 26 April 1919
from Florence

Your joy in the awakening spring at Bernardsville gave me a communicating thrill. How splendid for you to have these restful days there. The woods must be too enchanting now with the perfume of fresh leaves and embryo flowers – a carpet of moss – and the virgin sky with the wintry mantle of clouds thrown off.

Had a good day of tennis this afternoon at the club – pretty rusty after 3 years not playing, but it will come back. We must practise up and play some good doubles together. You used to have a very good stroke. Have just had two very amusing and chatty letters from George E. Brown – He has been away on a long tour with Alma Gluck and busy booking dates for the Wolfsohns for next season. He writes in his own characteristic style, saying: "You will certainly have a great season next year. Adams is tickled off his bean with the prospects so far and they sure are coming [along] – I think they have their guarantee of 50 concerts about set already and Adams told me they were further ahead with their books at this time than they usually are by May 15th" (His letter is dated April 2nd) – "Adams also said from present signs you could easily do 100 concerts next season – O Boy! That sure was some music to my ears – The only thing I want to complete my happiness is a second hand 'Flivver' to ride in & out from Jamaica!!!" and so on –

Poor old George Brown – as faithful and devoted as they make them. But I just quoted this as an indication of what the next season promises. But no 100 concerts for me. Too many by a long shot.

Just heard some reassuring news from White Star people in Genoa confirming that *Canopic* expects to sail from Genoa & Naples about May 15th – and promising accommodations, altho' not very good ones. Well! I don't care how poor the accommodations are so long as the sailing is assured.

Am still busy working on the Adagio of Sonate. Rewrote part of it today – and still am striking a snag. The Coda doesn't come properly – it lacks the flow it ought to have – "Yankee Doodle in Spain" is quite charming and a brilliant fiddle piece treated in modern spirit.

Yes! Your feeling that I have gone into another world is a very strange one – for I am nearer and nearer to your world – or you to mine – No, I am not absorbed with other things – I am absorbed by you. I do many things with zest because the thought of you constantly stimulates my interest in them. Have been writing music steadily, about 8 hours per day, sometimes more, but your image is floating over the notes. My stuff can never become commercial, I am better pleased that it doesn't — am not even looking for a publisher — The Sonate must wait and salt a bit anyway. There may be — probably will be many opportunities for the blue pencil — a beneficial dose of musical castor oil. I have now a nice theme in F sharp minor that should be adapted to variation in a free form. But that must wait until the Sonate is completed. Always on the lookout for nice poems for lyrics. English is really more of an intellectual form of poetry than a musical one. Sometimes difficult to suit the words with proper rhythms.

Tuesday, 29 April 1919
from Florence

The Adagio — is now entirely copied out and most successful, I *think*. There are two contrasting bold melodies (plantation) that sound deliciously fresh with the violin — and there are some novel effects to tone color. The piece is very difficult — and already I can see Benoist groaning over prospect of an intricate piano part. I am so happy that Trieste did not materialize as this extra time to myself has permitted completion of the Sonate. The last movement has less work to do, as it was already very thoroughly sketched in Rome. The form is all there — some polishing to be done, of course, but purposely I am leaving it rather naive and as far as possible blue pencilling all too involved kinks. There will be inversions of the Adagio themes and two of three reminiscences of 1st movement. It *is* a satisfaction and a pleasure to write in large form. More and more the ideas come easily. Can't wait to have you hear it and pass on it.

Excitement over political and diplomatic situation subsiding somewhat though there is still a considerable feeling over the affront which was so gratuitously offered to the Italian delegates. It is difficult to understand the reason for such a senseless piece of blundering and seems to have been quite unprecedented in the history of diplomacy. The effect here has been to weld together all elements — and Parliament registered an almost unanimous vote of confidence in Orlando, etc. My own impression is that from one standpoint, however, the Italian

Government is not altogether sorry for the political excitement and attending patriotic fervor of this incident to tide over the first days of May. The 1st of May in particular is sort of Labor Day in Italy and the Socialist and Bolshevist elements are expected to make a demonstration of some sort. The wind has been taken out of their sails, however, by this decision – and the few out and out anarchists will be a lonely company to each other. Patriotic excitement is bad propaganda for revolutionary discontent.

The weather still continues all-fired cold – imagine the end of April – in Florence and one freezes even with wood fires. Everyone has colds and sniffles. This, too, comes pretty hard on the poor people with coal at 600 lire a ton, and carbon coke about L. 350. Prices of all commodities still tremendously high – meat 12 lire a kilo – butter 10 lire a kilo – chickens go at almost any price. The purchasing power of money seems hopelessly crippled, unless one is a war profiteer – and "thank ye Marm" but that is, indeed too high a price on one's honor to pay for luxury or comfort.

Thursday, 1 May 1919
from Florence to Bernardsville, N.J.

Sweetheart: May 1st (the Ides of March!) is here, but not yet gone – So far everything quiet, and no terrifying demonstration of any kind. People are too much occupied with thoughts of a patriotic and nationalistic nature to do much worrying about revolutions and Bolshevism. Unless I am pretty mistaken the next few days are going to see this little diplomatic muddle cleared up. I had a very quiet day – wrote the last to the Sonata (the last movement) and the clean copy is now nearly completed. It's a sigh of relief to get it out of my system as already themes for a string quartette are haunting me and I am keen to jot them down. But this P.M. the sun came out and so at 5 o'clock I threw down the pen – got into white flannels and out to the tennis courts for three good sets of doubles. First time I've felt really warm for a week – for the phenomenally cold weather still continues and we have all our wood fires going. Very amusing political stories, but these are best not told on paper. O, if they will only make a straighforward, definite peace. Here we are nearly six months after the armistice – six months of futile and wandering discussions, enough to try the patience of Job.

Yes! my dearest, you *have* been much too appreciative, etc., of all the little commissions. You know what a joy it has been to me, any little thing I could do, and never for a moment imagine that it has been a trouble. Even if it had been a trouble (which it was not), I should have loved doing them. So banish all vain scruples from your mind. I have tried, but in vain to procure the Debussy songs here and had them write to Milan. Not time to obtain them from Paris as mail – and especially parcel post takes forever – even now.

Was interested in what you say of Marcia van Dresser. I never heard her sing, but have met her several times – always charmed by her personality, quite a style of beauty of her own, don't you think? She was a great friend of Loretta del Valle, a singer who assisted me in some of the concerts I had in Cuba and elsewhere. Del Valle had a very hard time and I was intensely sorry for her as she was a good singer and a very decent woman (perhaps this stood in her way from an operatic standpoint) but she simply could not get over the foot-lights. I used to have the same sensation of the sub-conscious effort one invariably makes for a motor of insufficient horse-power climbing a hill – Requiescat in pace!

Too bad the songs never reached you – though I haven't yet given up hope. I mailed them from Milano, March 25th or 26th and one should reasonably allow three weeks or more – extra grave to some poor censor who imagines he can decode a cypher – Well!! The only cypher he'll find there is one of infinite love for my precious darling – Ever and ever – *Your own adoring Albert* –

Saturday, 3 May 1919
from Florence to Bernardsville, N. J.

How well I understand that "dumb" feeling when there is so much to say. But why my darling is thus afflicted is a mystery to me. You have so wonderfully that power of expression – few people have it – and you on the contrary have it to such a degree. Your letters always give me the impression that I've been chatting with you and I become immediately stimulated – it even makes the bread taste better. I am just waiting to have my passage actually in hand and paid for before cabling you the definite sailing. Feel almost superstitious about it. Please give your mother my dear love and tell her what a pleasure it will be to meet any of her family (& yours, dearest!) and her friends it will be for me . . . But, sweet, Beloved! I shall be more nervous than for ten concerts, probably spill the tea and walk on the lace dresses. You'll have to advise as to color of neck-tie, and am I to say "Yes, Marm" – or "Sure! Madam!" when spoken to. I have been leading such a hermit's life here in Florence.

The last movement of the Sonate all copied out – neat & fresh – some work – 49 pages (the whole) and closely written. Aside from this have been copying out another of the Acquarelles – a Gavotte Caprice and sketching the orchestration of the Concerto. The String Quartette still in abeyance. That must wait and ripen some. Am getting my things slowly put away and packed . . . Yes! Dearest – appearances are certainly against me and perhaps I merit the appellation slow-moving snail – (but please) remember however the fable of the race between the Hare and the Turtle – The Hare all speed at first, but the Turtle is the steady goer and reaches the goal first while the Hare is sleeping off the effects of his violent but short-lived exuberance. But this, by the way – For I give you fair warning that I intend to usurp all your time, attention, tenderness, beauty, wit, charm, grace, etc., etc. – No, you have not got green eyes – I protest. They are hazel – grey rainbow color with violet tints!

The little green stone has come home and looks quite attractive, I think. Enfin on peut toujours l'arranger come tu voudras.

Monday, 5 May 1919
from Florence to Bernardsville, N. J.

The *Canopic* was due in Genoa today, but arrived instead, at Naples so I hear – Genoa tomorrow or Wednesday. It should be ready to leave again by the 15th, or 16th, or 17th. Shouldn't take that long, but docking facilities aren't all they should be and with so much cargo to unload now it takes double the appointed time. We are to have quite comfortable accommodations which is remarkable – only 2 in a room – Father & I – Mother & Stella Traverso. If only they don't hold us up at Gibralter too long. But we have a far better chance of not having the delay with an English than an Italian boat – on account of the English control of Gibraltar. Had a rather embarrassing task today. A letter from a Russian lady – Princess Obolensky – she is daughter to Alexander IInd of Russia by his morganatic marriage with Princess Ysurieff. Escaped the Bolshevicki and arrived at Nice practically penniless.

Believes she has a chance to make her living by means of her voice — as everyone looks to America as an Eldorado & proposes to try her luck there and writes for all possible information — Well! I wrote as frankly and kindly as possible, but it wasn't easy. Poor woman, she doesn't realize what she's going to strike. My suggestion was for her to capitalize on her social position and come well munitioned with letters of introduction to important families — and content herself at first with private engagements at first and if they go well, then venture to other things. There is a certain set that is just foolish and snobbish enough to fall for it if it's presented in the proper way. Besides, it appears she is quite beautiful which ought to help matters along. Haven't the faintest idea whether she can sing or not.

The anticipation of actually seeing you again in persona seems too, too wonderful. After all, life *is* worth living for such moments — and even now I have the thrills — thrills enough to sustain a movie scenario — with you as star actress!!!!! Was pleased to see Senator Lodge's declarations concerning Fiume and the Italians. He does think and talk so straight. No cloudy vagaries. The air has been made so foggy with generalities that it is refreshing to hear anything clear cut, either pro or contra. A letter from Benoist confirms Brown's reports as to prospects of next season. Wolfsohn is evidently presenting it very properly — The N. Y. Symphony is the opening concert — then comes a tour of the Pacific Coast — Brown says January, Benoist — November — then Boston Symphony, N.Y. Philharmonic, Chicago Symphony, Philadelphia Orchestra — St.Louis — Minneapolis, etc. and 1st New York recital scheduled for near Xmas time. Benoist is now down in the little Monmouth Beach home which he has bought — one long wail about my delayed return. I think he is happy to be rid of Papa & Mama Heifetz tho' he likes the boy, and certainly it has been an excellent berth for him during my absence. Was delighted to hear that Scott had been working again on a picture of you. Am tremendously keen to see his last work. It had already developed so finely when I last saw it — admired especially the portrait of himself — Spanish in style which I saw one day on exhibition at the 5th Avenue place.

Saturday, 10 May 1919
from Florence to Bernardsville, then forwarded to 375 Park Ave.

And actually the last — is it possible? Am almost superstitious about stopping to write. Sent you a cable, dearest, precising the sailing date as the 17th, but it may be a day or two later than that,will cable again from Genoa or Naples when we've actually sailed. Am so enchanted you liked the little songs — anyway it was a real labor of love — and all inspired by my darling — Met Guigliemo Ferrero, the great historian, on Saturday — do you know his wonderful book "Between the Old World and the New"? Like all (really) big people he is intensely simple, speaks with great pleasure of his visit to America & lectures at the universities. His wife, a quaint figure, looks like a portrait [by] Bronzino. Her father was Lumbroso the Criminologist. They came in yesterday evening when we had a little music.

Monday, 23 May 1919
from Albergo Palazzo Roma to 375 Park Ave.

Dearest: My cable Saturday must have been as great a bomb-shell to you as it was to me to send. Imagine — on the eve of sailing our trunks packed, passports visa-ed, when telegraphic communications from Genova White Star Line notified that British Gov't. has suddenly and without previous warning requisitioned boat — many people are thrown out of passage — needless to speak to you of my feelings. They were best translated into action. We sent a man immediately to Genoa to endeavor by all means for passage on *Dante* sailing the 27th — also telegraphed France for possibilities of passage from there. In the meantime, have come here to Rome — Father and I — to do what we could thru official circles — The *Dante*, of course, has been booked solid with Army and Red Cross for months — but all wires are being pulled to obtain a possible release of 2 cabins — The *Pesaro* sails too late in June, but there are still other boats if *Dante* fails and at all events we have gained the assurance from Embassy that they will visa our passports from France provided we can obtain passage from there. This is an extraordinary concession, but I have represented the urgency of the case — and everything possible is being done — my only comfort is in this constant action and I *will achieve results*. Both Mother and Father feel dreadfully about it and sympathetic, aside from the anxiety Father

James Walter Spalding.

has of being so long away from business. Only this much I can write — every possible effort is being strained, every channel used and the legitimacy of our claim has found more official support than I dared hope for. The wires are kept busy and by tomorrow or next day I hope to cable you brighter news. In the meantime, dearest, make plans *for what you wish to do* and I will conform to them. This is only fair and due to you and your mother, besides it is my happiness to concur in your wishes. Am returning to Florence tonight — where we should find an answer from France and the Embassy promises news tomorrow or next day regarding *Dante* or future Italian sailings previous to *Pesaro*. The delay in *Pesaro* upset many things, too. She does not sail till after June 15th — was first scheduled for end of May or early June. If I felt less keenly I could write more freely of how this has affected me. Even up till the last ten days I had some misgivings about the *Canopic*, but the last reassurances from the company were so definite — our staterooms assigned and everything O.K. that I was totally unprepared for this last eventuality. Talk about seeing stars! I saw 'em by the million when that telegram came. I am not over-sanguine over the *Dante* possibilities altho' the Embassy has made a very strong appeal for an exception in our case – and it may be that Father & I can sail – or I alone in case passage can not be obtained for Mother. Well! We are doing what we can and from all wires pulled *something must happen*. The fact that our passports can be amended for France is a great comfort – as that gives another chance –

Editor's Note: Between May 23 and June 28 obviously passage from Italy to the States was obtained and a reunion took place – When? Where? (No records found.)

Monday, 30 June 1919
from Florenzia, Monmouth Beach, N. J.
to The Elms, Ridgefield, Conn.

Dearest: Such a hectic day! Called on Mr. Leask [Pyle family lawyer], enjoyed meeting him a really charming old Gentleman. He said things to make your ears burn. Of course, I hotly disputed with him! Then to Mr. MacMillin's – He was most agreeable to the idea of Beaver Island, altho' a number of things must be done to make the place liveable, such as rescreening, cleaning, mending docks, etc., etc. But he is writing forthwith and will have an answer in a week's time as to cost, etc. – Thinks the place might be ready August 1st and is delighted to have us occupy it. Then I went to Tiffany and ordered the envelopes and die of crest made. Saw Mr. Moise and he assured me you would have the envelopes not later than tomorrow. Die will take some little time – ought to be ready next week though – cost approx. 22 dollars. Your mother had thought 27 so I thought safe to order. Is this O. K.? Then I called at 5 East 53rd, Miss Lawton not there but sign said to call on Barry (who are her agents). This I did. He told me, only one back floor apt. (2 rooms) was available for rent. I had already seen this & saw at once that it would not do at all. I was also to several other apartments, but not much success in that line. Hope to see something tomorrow. In all events I do think it most important to settle on something – or some definite plan before leaving for Maine – Don't you think that if we are going to take an apt., it should be something attractive even if more be paid for it? Otherwise, better hold off for a season and content ourselves with hotel rooms. This last, of course, does not appeal to me so much. However, we'll thrash this all out on Thursday when I see my darling again. I think it is going to prove very difficult to crowd all these things in before July 19th, but am willing to make a stab for it, if you wish—But in view of August 1st for Island—(not ready before)—prudence is fighting with my impatience to counsel the August 3rd date (wasn't that the other one you suggested) as more practical. But this is entirely up to you, my darling, and I shall abide by your decision.

Wednesday, 9 July 1919
from Florenzia to Ridgefield, Conn.

My beloved: It was a furious rush to make the train as the Presidential procession held up the crowds on 5th Avenue at a great length. Well! He's home, let's hope he'll stay "put" for a while! The more I think of it the more I feel we've been wise not to rush into either apt. venture half-baked. I have a feeling that the LaSalle Chambers are going to work out O. K. You are simply adorable. Don't tire yourself out—and don't worry over anything, It's going to be smooth sailing—and we can always rely on our sense of humor for the tight places. If we can't accomplish everything at double speed time, that's no cause for unhappiness. I tried to quote you something from Lincoln yesterday—but was too hectic to do it properly. It was from his first inaugural address: "If there be any object to hurry any of you in hot haste to a step which you would never take deliberately, that object will be frustrated by taking time, but *no good object* can be frustrated by taking time." Seems to me this could be applied equally well to the League of Nations and also to our rushing almost blindfolded into apartments.

There were notices today in both Sun and Tribune, quite respectable ones. At all events I'm pleased that there's been nothing sensational or offensive.

Wednesday, 16 July 1919
from New York City to Ridgefield

Darling—Am thinking of you day and night—each hour brings us nearer, closer together—I am so happy and you have been wonderfully sweet to give me the conviction of your dear happiness. Am struggling like a Trojan to get everything accomplished—had MacMillin send wire to say that if Ellingwood wouldn't cook, I could take care of the cooking end. Will see him tomorrow. In the meantime, have talked to Irene and will see her tomorrow—Gov. Clement's lodge is available in

Vermont. May be advisable to see it—before we decide—We could easily motor there from Manchester, Vermont. Have sent wires for accommodations to Lenox, Great Barrington, and to Manchester for the 2nd stop. Asked to have answers sent to The Elms which you can open. Attended to Tiffany's and gave instructions concerning not marking silver—O dear! I do hope I shan't forget anything—But if I do you'll just have to be indulgent—and remember, I adore you—*Toujours à toi* ALBERT

From *Rise to Follow,* in his own words:

Mary Pyle and I were married on July 19, 1919. It was a quiet wedding in the little white church at Ridgefield, Connecticut. Mary was as opposed as I to making this intimate event a public spectacle so only our families and a very few friends were at the church. Music by Jacques Thibaud, with André Benoist at the organ, was a delightful wedding present.

We spent our honeymoon in a white frame cottage in the village of Mendon, Vermont—the epitome of shabby comfort. We were taken care of by a general house servant, Mary Flynn, as Irish as the shamrock. Once or twice a week we would drive the four miles to Rutland for provisions. There were long practice hours in the morning, picnic teas in the afternoon. A nearby lake, the town reservoir, was a favorite spot. We could canoe to a miniature island in the center and, while Mary boiled water for tea, I would disturb the peace by stripping for an icy plunge. Evenings we spent reading aloud to each other. These outwardly uneventful days may not sound exciting, but they are an excellent recipe for contentment.

The summer ended all too soon.

Coda

THE ARDUOUS music season of 1919-20 followed and included the historic European tour of the New York Symphony, led by Walter Damrosch with Albert Spalding, violinist-composer, and John Powell, composer-pianist, as the two accompanying artists. In *Rise to Follow,* Albert wrote of the great reception in honor of Camille Saint-Saens at the Institut de France and his delight with Mary, in her new Callot gown, together with three of the Damrosch daughters.

The pattern of his concert life resumed. With three to four months abroad and four to five months touring America, only three months a year were spent at home together. In the twenties, Mary often went abroad with him but usually stayed in Paris or Florence, or another major city, attending only his most important concerts. She accompanied him, too, on some of his American tours when they were first married, but after they had established a home in New York City and later in the Berkshires, she usually remained at home, or met Albert for some special occasion and for side trips on their own.

They spent summer holidays together in England in the early years, and later summers high in the pines at Aston Magna, in Great Barrington, Massachusetts, which they lovingly developed together. Both enjoyed swimming and were avid tennis players. He was known locally as the club champion. Many evenings by their fireside, they read aloud to each other. Their mutual interest in books, the arts, and nature grew even deeper. Albert had a passion for Shakespeare and always traveled with one of the plays, the Bible, and some current literature. Here at Aston Magna they indulged their interests and built notable collections of books, ceramics, English antiques, and Chinese objets d'art.

These months of relaxation were also very productive for composing and working on new programs for the coming season. He is credited with sixty works for violin, twenty-five for piano, thirty for voice, four for chamber ensemble, and four cadenzas for concerti.

Radio was coming into its own in the twenties. Albert appeared early on the first popular Atwater Kent Hour and later as a frequent guest on other fine music programs. The publicity value of these "concerts-on-the-air" was immediately reflected in increased concert engagements and the sale of his records. America was awakening to music everywhere and he was an important part of that awakening by touring extensively and regularly throughout the United States, bringing fine music to small cities and towns as well as to the metropolitan centers, in recitals and orchestral appearances. During that decade he played in thirty-one states and in more than one hundred twenty-five towns and cities, with annual or biennial repeats in most of them. And wherever he found aspiring young American violinists, he listened, encouraged, and advised them. A few became his private pupils, or were coached at Juilliard, where he taught for over twelve years.

Mary and Albert's separations and reunions were a part of the pattern of his life as a world-renowned concert artist. They had been conditioned to it for almost a decade and lived it continuously and harmoniously after their marriage for thirty-five years, until his sudden untimely death in May 1953. Their daily letters to each other when apart attest to their abiding love and tenderness — and their many shared interests. Mary lived on at Aston Magna until 1971.

En route Chicago: November 21, 1926

Sweetheart: Just a line of love and sinking sense of depression at the putting of miles of railroad between us. I have not wanted to think about it all these last days — these last dear hours, every one of which I treasure up and cherish.

There is a quality of love which spells perfect fulfillment and this, bless you, is the love which you know how to give and how to inspire. And it is this, this above all, which makes of our fireside such a tonic chord of all that the world can hold dear. And it's the consciousness and conviction of this very thing which sustains an abiding sense of your presence — never allows me to feel completely separated, which evokes a word, a smile, a caress simultaneously with the poignant pang of physical absence. I can conceive of no state of Heaven without you there to share it, for you hold the keys to all the closed doors of my heart and mind. Ton Albert qui t'adore.

As he departs for service in World War II – again in the Italian Campaign –

March 13, 1944.

Sweetheart: Just a line to greet you, I hope tomorrow morning. There is no good-bye – there never is – because between us is an invisible link stronger and more certain than anything fashioned by the hand of man. You give me – have given – and are giving twenty-five years of perfect happiness. One can write this even when one can't say it. I am glad the last glimpse on the street had an abrupt closing. You understood, and so did I that everything was said and was there. You're by my side, now and always. Don't worry! Don't worry! Don't worry! And don't let anyone suggest worrying to you. Avoid it like poison – I'll not let you down! Everything is relaxed and serene. I'm going forth with an humble consciousness of my limitations, but you'll be there as an inspiration when I have to improvise. All blessings, all love – Albert

Albert Spalding

Illustrations and Credits

In the following all illustrations appearing in this volume are listed sequentially with the abbreviated caption followed by the name of the photographer or delineator where known, and the page on which it appears. It should be noted that all the photographs included are in the Albert Spalding Collection of Boston University Libraries.

Ton Albert qui t'adore

has been published in a first edition
of one thousand copies.
Designed by A. L. Morris,
the text was composed in Paladium
and printed by Sherwin/Dodge, Printers,
in Littleton, New Hampshire
on Monadnock Caress Text.
The binding, in Holliston Mills Roxite,
was executed by New Hampshire Bindery
in Concord, New Hampshire.

now – another
and then I a
– you, the ne
with that loo
which gives m
joy – And al
fall about u
Toyou
a